For Peggy Lee

Acknowledgements:

One of the fundamental tenets of prosperity is that we can accomplish many good things as individuals, but in order to accomplish a great thing that can touch many others, we need help from others.

With that thought in mind, I would like to thank....

...Valerie Lancaster for her formatting and layout skills
...Shannon Arriola for her eagle-eye editing and proofing skills
...Andrew Black for his cover design skills

Prosperity: Having It Living It
HOW TO BE, DO, AND HAVE WHAT YOU WANT IN LIFE

TABLE OF CONTENTS

Forward:	A Note From The Author
Segment One:	Money Isn't The Root Of Anything Unless You Decide It Is
Segment Two:	The Starting Point For Everything Is Desire
Segment Three:	Deciding What You Want: You've Got To Do It
Segment Four:	Programming For Success Is A Choice: So Is Programming for Less Than Success
Segment Five:	Persistence Pays Of In Many Ways
Segment Six:	"Ideas" Everybody Has Them . . . Properous People Use Them
Segment Seven:	It May Be Lonely At The Top Sometimes, But Getting There Never Is
Afterword:	Another Note From The Author

Prosperity: Having It Living It
How To Be, Do, and Have What You Want In Life

ISBN-13:978-1-937659-04-2
Copyright © 2012 By Jim Johnson
MIE Institute
HC 70 Box 3172
Sahuarita, AZ 85629
www.themieinstitute.com

Cover Photo: Thinkstock

All rights reserved, including the right of reproduction in whole or part in any form.

FORWARD

A Note from Jim Johnson

As I write this, I'm looking out from an ocean-view balcony at a hotel in Porto Roma, the Port of Rome. My wife Peggy and I are here to spend the last night of our trip before flying back to our home after a 26-day Transatlantic/Mediterranean cruise. The rhythm of the ocean waves is constant and gentle, and one can't look out over this bright, sunny beach without feeling lucky to be here enjoying it.

There are a number of restaurants where you can enjoy an ocean view along with your dining experience, like the one we visited yesterday for a lingering afternoon lunch of spaghetti, light oil and vinegar salad, bread, and a bottle of wine. Afterward, we strolled down the clean, quiet, store-front lined street near our hotel, and enjoyed a small cup of dessert we chose from among a variety of flavors at a nearby Galateria....the equivalent of a Mom & Pop ice cream store in the United States.

Tonight, we'll chill a bottle of wine we purchased at a small shop where the proprietor's English wasn't much better than my Italian, but we still had fun picking out the one we wanted, and we'll relax as we watch the full moon come up as though it's supposed to be doing it in secret.

Stop. Think. How do you feel about what you just read? Were you enjoying my story, or were you feeling uncomfortable because you thought it was just something being written simply to impress you? (Or, maybe you were thinking, "Wow, these people drink too much wine," which we don't. It's just that if you're in Italy, there's so much good wine to enjoy at a wonderful price, you want to take advantage of the situation.)

If you were enjoying my story, that's good. If you found yourself leaning more toward the uncomfortable slant I mentioned, that's still OK, it just means we have some work to do together.

Let me make one thing clear. No, I'm not telling you about a stay in the Port of Rome to impress you. All I'm saying is that for everyone, prosperity means different things. To us, it sometimes means taking vacation time and spending it on a cruise ship, which, by the way is often much less expensive that people guess it is. Often, people harbor the belief that they "can't afford".... (if you take only one piece of information away from reading this, vow to never utter those words again) ...to take a cruise.

For some, that erroneous and limiting idea is based on the opinion that cruises are only for the elite. While that might have been true to some extent in decades past, it certainly isn't true today. Cruising on a luxury ship and enjoying fine dining every night, along with all your other meals included in the price, is within the reach of anyone who really wants to experience it.

What's that? You say you're just barely getting along as it is and you have no money left over for any kind of vacation, much less an ocean cruise?

Well, that might be true for you at the moment, but it doesn't have to stay that way. If you *truly* set your mind to the fact that you absolutely want to go on a cruise, you'll figure out a way to get it done, whether it means saving the money for it by giving up your daily $5 latte or taking a weekend job and earmarking all of the revenue from it for nothing but a cruise vacation. Notice the emphasis on the *truly* in the above sentence. That's one of the things we'll be covering in this book. But for now, I just want to emphasize the idea that for us, experiencing prosperity is many things, and one of them happens to be taking a cruise.

For you, it might be different. You might decide that experiencing true prosperity involves climbing into a modified, high-performance SUV that you practically need a ladder to get into, and challenging yourself by proving your driving skills in the roughest terrain you can find. Or maybe your idea of true prosperity doesn't have anything to do with going anywhere or doing anything.

Perhaps it's just enjoying being surrounded by your family, happy and healthy. Whatever your idea of having and living prosperity is, the purpose of this book is to help you find a way to have and live it. And the first step to achieving what you want in the realm of having and living prosperity is to understand how your beliefs either allow, or prevent you from doing so.

"SOMETIMES THE LARGEST PART OF LEARNING IS NOT GATHERING NEW INFORMATION, BUT GETTING RID OF OLD BELIEFS."

I made that statement at the opening of a prosperity workshop I facilitated a few years ago, and at the first break, a man in his fifties approached me and said that it was the most profound thing anyone had ever said to him in his entire lifetime. While I was happy that he took the time to tell me that, I wasn't surprised. I'm convinced that many people that I've worked with over the years, while they haven't taken the time to tell me about it as that gentleman did, get quite a whack on the side of the head when I mention this concept. As human beings, we sometimes overlook the simplest ideas.

This is the underpinning of any practical prosperity teaching philosophy. Before I can get you to absorb (and honestly accept and embrace) new information, we have to decide together if it matches your old information, and if the new stuff will "fit" into your belief system. If it doesn't fit, then the above quote describes the process we'll go through together.

And, the reason that we'll have to go through that, I believe, is because our overall exposure to the learning process. Our educational system, primarily conditions us to be information gatherers, going from classroom to classroom from *whosaid* to *whosaid* at the front of the room. What's a *whosaid*? That's the high school teacher, or community college instructor, university professor, or seminar leader is at the front of the room.

When we walk into their room to spend the school year, semester, or the day with them, we're conditioned to try and grab onto and take with us as much of their new information as possible, before leaving to go on to the next *whosaid's* room.

The challenge this creates for us as life-long students…and that is what we are, each and every one of us… is that we grow and change constantly. Which means that sometimes information we accepted as gospel ten years ago just doesn't fit with what we're learning today, and a great deal of effort can be expended trying to make everything "fit" together.

It can be difficult to let go of things. Our society conditions us as gatherers and keepers. The idea of hanging on to everything while trying to gather some more is one of the concepts that is diametrically opposed to having what can be referred to simply as a prosperity consciousness.

And the idea of hanging on to things is not limited to possessions. It also applies to knowledge. And if some new knowledge doesn't meld with the old stuff, we sometimes have a tendency to bounce around from thought to thought, while we struggle to make sense of it all. Having a prosperity consciousness means not struggling. It also means not stubbornly hanging onto knowledge and beliefs that are no longer valid, no matter how much time, money and effort we invested in gathering the knowledge, and then developing our beliefs based on that knowledge.

Now, with that point made, it's time to address some questions that might have occurred to you while you're considering buying this book.

Question: Does this book have a lot of religious stuff in it? Is that where this consciousness stuff comes from? Are you going to try and shove God and Jesus down my throat and tell me that if I'll just be a better person than I am now, I'll be rich beyond my wildest dreams?

Answer: Actually, that's three questions. The answer is no to all of them.

Question: Are you an MLM guy who's using your book as an avenue to recruit and expand your Down-line?

Answer: No… nor do I sell franchises, head up an insurance company, or have a formula you can get fabulously rich with in real estate. Those things don't fit into my mission. I will say that there are lots of people who do those things very well, and if connecting with them is your road to prosperity, so be it. It's just not what I do.

Question: Are you going to use a lot of paper and ink, or data space on my e-reader, explaining to me that the reason I don't have everything I want in life as far as relationships, money, or the job I want is because I subconsciously hate my mother?

Answer: Wow… that one really came in from way out in left field….but, no. However, as long as we're on the subject, I will say that a lot of the wrong thinking we do about prosperity comes from the environment we were raised in but, our parents, bless their hearts, were, like all parents, doing the best job they knew how with us, so there's no reason to waste any time blaming them for anything.

Question: Oh, so that's it….the child thing. Are you going to tell me how "finding the child within" is the answer to happiness in life?

Answer: The only thing I know about children within relates to a pregnant woman. So, that's another no.

Question: Well, if the answer to all of these questions is no, then what are you going to do for me?

Answer: I'm going to be giving you information that I truly believe you can use to achieve total prosperity in your life. I'll also present ideas so you can decide which ones fit for you and which ones don't…and put the ones you decide to embrace into practice.

Now that we have all of your questions answered, I want to thank you for giving me the opportunity to be a part of your growth, learning and happiness. Here's hoping that I will either say something you consider to be the most profound thing you've ever heard in your life, or lead you to someone else who will say it to you. As Mr. Spock used to say, "May you live long and prosper.

NOTES:

SEGMENT ONE

**MONEY ISN'T THE ROOT OF ANYTHING
UNLESS YOU DECIDE IT IS**

SEGMENT ONE
MONEY ISN'T THE ROOT OF ANYTHING UNLESS YOU DECIDE IT IS

Lots of people have read lots of prosperity books. That's because there are lots of people who want to know what prosperity is all about, and there are lots of prosperity books available. So, lots of people have read lots of prosperity books. Lots of people have also participated in lots of prosperity workshops and listened to lots of prosperity audio programs. And, often, while people are reading the books, listening to the CD's or downloads, or attending the workshops, there's an issue (actually, it would be better described as an entity) that, while it's in the back of their mind, is at the forefront of their concern.

If this entity could talk, here's what it would say while it waited patiently (somewhat) to get through the first chapters of the book or audio program, or workshop segments.....

"Oh, yes, I agree, relationships are important."

" Uh, huh, taking the time to enjoy my children is true prosperity. And, oh, yes, if I'm happy in my work, that's an important part of achieving total prosperity."

" Yes, yes, yes, true happiness is achieved within. I'm in complete agreement with that....umm, when do we get to the part about money?"

If we've offended you with this segment introduction, at least you have to admit that we did the offending very early, which means that now we can get on with the business at hand, which is helping you "get it." Not just money, we mean, but "it."

It's not our intent to offend by insinuating that you're greedy, selfish, shallow, or materialistic. It's just that we honestly want people to get it. The unfortunate truth is that many people invest a lot of years struggling, and engaging in a lot of negative experiences, because they just don't 'get' it. We want you to get it. However, the reality is that in order for you to get it, you've got to pay attention. And you can't pay attention if you're thinking about something else while we're trying to help you get *it*. So let's get this money stuff out of the way right now. That way, you'll be able to concentrate. And you'll get it.

THE UNFORTUNATE TRUTH IS THAT MANY PEOPLE INVEST A LOT OF YEARS STRUGGLING, AND ENGAGING IN A LOT OF NEGATIVE EXPERIENCES, BECAUSE THEY JUST DON'T 'GET' IT.

To begin, we'll address some of the junk that's in the consciousness of many people when they think about money. Some of the junk may be of a religious nature, or some of it may be from early exposure to information from parents or other adults. Or, some of it may be drawn from negative experiences in your adult life. The one we'll tackle first is the phrase that's most commonly misquoted…"Money is the root of all evil."

The correct quote is, "The LOVE of money is the root of evil."

In other words, if a person loves money more than they love their family, they're in a sad state of affairs. If they love money more than they care about doing things for others, then they need to re-evaluate their priorities. If money is the one and only thing that keeps a person in a given job or position, then they've got a serious problem because they're either obsessed with money or believe they're trapped by the need for money…actually harboring an incorrect belief about the availability of money. The quote doesn't say that money itself is an evil thing that brings about the downfall of a greedy person. What it says is that becoming obsessed with money is the problem.

"Wait a minute, here," you might be thinking at this moment. "Money is important. While the old Beatles song *All You Need Is Love* may be fun to listen to, we have to face reality here. If you don't have money, you can't have your own house to live in, a car to drive, or even food to eat. Money is important!"

And, we agree. Money is important. You're absolutely right that mortgage or rent payments take money. To buy a car, insure it, maintain it, and put gas in it, you need money. When you go to the grocery store, the people operating the cash registers don't ask you to tell them how much you love you family, care about doing a good job or providing service to others. What they *do* ask for is some money in exchange for the eggs, bread, milk, vegetables, pizza, or whatever items you have put in your cart and intend to take home with you.

We all exchange money for the things we want and need. No argument there. And the most common method we employ to get our hands on the money we give in exchange for the things we want and need is to exchange some of our time and expertise for money. And the idea of exchange is a fundamental idea we want to focus on. That's all money is, a tool for exchange. It's not something we should obsess about. A dollar bill, a five, ten, twenty or a hundred is just paper and ink, not a mysterious, elusive thing we're supposed to worship, squeeze, or worry about. It's just a tool. And to prove that money shouldn't be mysterious, we want to present some fundamental details about it.

The dollar is the most recognized currency in the world, and the reason we call a dollar a dollar is because the term "Leeuwendaalders"….which eventually evolved to Liondollars….was introduced in the 17th century by the Dutch. And "daalder", (actually derived from the German "thaler"), became "dollar" when a coin equivalent to the Spanish eight-reales coin, popular with colonists, was first referred to as a Spanish Dollar.

Whew….that was a long-winded explanation, wasn't it? A Dutch term, which was actually a German term, which eventually became an American term, because of a Spanish coin? Well, as convoluted as it may sound, that's how the term we use today came about.

And there's also no mystery as to why we use the symbol "$" to identify dollars. In the early days of the United States, a typewriter would be used to type the letter "U", then the machine would be backspaced, and the "S" typed over it to identify the "US" dollar. Eventually, the symbol became a hand-written "S" with two lines through to represent the original "U".

Have you ever taken a close look at a dollar bill? If you haven't taken the time to do that, do it now.

Start on the front, the side where George Washington is looking out at us from that ornate picture frame. On this side of the dollar, it says simply that it's a Federal Reserve Note and that it's "legal tender for all debts, public and private." There are also letters and numbers that identify the bill in more specific terms. Things like a serial number and a letter designating a series. There is also what is known as the Great Seal of The United States, bearing the information "The Department of The Treasury" with a date of 1789.

The date 1789 identifies the year of the creation of the Treasury Department. The seal also shows balance scales that represent justice, a key that is the emblem of official authority, and what is known as a chevron (no, not the gas station people) that contains thirteen stars. The number represents the thirteen original states.

On the back of the dollar, there are several symbols that have been the subject of debate, conjecture, conspiracy theories, confusion, and question. It's not the numbers, or even the "In God We Trust" that generates most of the controversy and question, it's the item that is actually the reverse side (the image on the front of the dollar bill is on what is known as the obverse) of the Great Seal of The United States.

The Great Seal was officially adopted in 1782 and was designed by a committee headed by Benjamin Franklin, Thomas Jefferson and John Adams. It was only used on official documents early in America's history, but eventually fell into obscurity. It first appeared on the dollar bill in 1935 after an aide to President Franklin Roosevelt re-discovered it and suggested that its symbolism would be a good fit for the design of our money.

Both sides of the seal are shown on the back of the dollar. The side that's described as the obverse side is on the right, and the side identified as the reverse is shown on the left. The obverse shows an American eagle, and it is breasted by the national shield of the United States. In its right talon, the eagle holds an olive branch of thirteen leaves and thirteen berries. These represent peace. In its left talon, the eagle holds thirteen arrows, which are intended to signify the original colonies' fight for liberty.

There is a ribbon in the eagle's beak and it is inscribed with the Latin motto "E Pluribus Unum" which translates to "one out of many." This inscription refers to the unity of the thirteen colonies as one government. And, on the illustration of the seal, there is also a constellation of thirteen five-pointed stars surrounded by a wreath of clouds, and a shield with thirteen bars, two more references to the unity of the colonies and the original thirteen states.

The side of the seal that depicts the eagle doesn't generate much controversy, but the other side of the seal…well, that's a different story.

Many things have been said about the pyramid and the eye above it. According to the Treasury Department, the pyramid represents permanence in strength, and its unfinished condition tells us that there is still work to be done in order to form a more perfect union. The eye above the pyramid, again according to the Treasury Department, is an "eye in the triangular glory" and it represents an all-seeing Deity. The Latin words "annuit coeptus" are taken to mean that "He (meaning the Deity...God) has favored our undertakings." Our founding fathers considered it important to make reference to what they described as the influence of Divine Providence in forming our government.

The other Latin phrase on this side of the seal, "novus ordo seciourum" translates to "a new order of the ages" and is intended to signify and new American era. At the base of the pyramid the Roman Numerals MDCCLXXVI, which represents the year 1776, the year of the Declaration of Independence, are inscribed.

Aside from the Treasury Department explanations, there are other organizations that have their own opinions as to what the pyramid, the Latin phrases and the "eye in the triangular glory" represent. Some Christian-based organizations contend that the eye is shown surrounded by sunbeams and inside a triangle with its apex pointed upward as a symbol of divine omnipresence, meaning that God is ever-present everywhere. And some religious organizations claim that the eye on the back of the dollar is part of a sinister plot.

There are also claims that this same plot instigated the French Revolution, inspired Marx and Engels to write The Communist Manifesto, and that it has something to do with the assassination of Abraham Lincoln. Many people also believe that there is some kind of Freemason conspiracy related to the design of the Great American Seal and its appearance on the dollar bill.

An explanation offered by the Masons refers to the "all-seeing eye" as something to remind them of the soul's immortality, which will be complete in eternity. Mason explanations of the symbols also say that the incomplete pyramid represents the unfinished temple of Solomon, which wasn't completed due to the fact that the master architect was killed. Other Masonic explanations are that the pyramid represents the Masonic philosophy that Freemasonry began in ancient times.

Whatever theory you ascribe to, be it the non-sectarian description by the Treasury Department, a spiritual approach, Masonry, or whatever, the point of our description of the dollar bill was to accomplish one simple thing. And that was to demystify it for you.

Like we said, it's a tool that is used for exchange. We get it in exchange for our time and service to others, and then we use it as an exchange for goods and services from others. It's nothing more than ink and paper, not something to be angry about if it seems that others around you have more of it than you do, or to worry over. Through the ages, many different commodities have been used as money: salt, pepper and other spices, shells, and even "coins" made of limestone that could be nine to twelve feet in diameter, weighing up to several tons.

To take an even further step toward demystifying money, consider the term itself. Why do we call money, "money?" The word we use today is derived from the term "Moneta." It originated in ancient Rome and related to the minting of coins. The ancient Roman Mint was established in the temple of the goddess Juno, formally referred to as the Temple Juno Moneta…hence the evolution of the term we use today.

And, speaking of our money in this day and age, consider the simple system under which our money was traditionally issued a value. For a time in our history, all the money that was minted or printed was backed up by precious metals stored in vaults.

"A DOLLAR BILL, A FIVE, TEN, TWENTY OR A HUNDRED IS JUST PAPER AND INK, NOT A MYSTERIOUS, ELUSIVE THING WE'RE SUPPOSED TO WORSHIP, SQUEEZE, OR WORRY ABOUT. IT'S JUST A TOOL."

Imagine for a moment that during that time frame, somebody stole all the gold or silver, but nobody knew about the theft. In a monetary system based on believing that the gold and silver that supported it was stored away safely, and the belief that the gold was always safely stored away remained in spite of the theft – even if it wasn't there in the vaults – nothing would have changed in the way that money (paper and ink or coins) was used as a medium of exchange.

Today, our money is considered to have what is known as "fiat value" because it has no backing and would be totally worthless if our society didn't continue to use and accept it as if it still had backing in precious metals.

Now that we've demystified the dollar for you, consider another simple, yet important idea. If you are harboring any negative thoughts about money, there is a simple exercise you can do to free yourself of these thoughts. Take a dollar bill and get rid of it. Burn it if you want, cut it up and put it in the cat litter, put it in a paper shredder, or take whatever creative steps please you. But get rid of it.

And when we say get rid of it, we really mean get rid of it. Throwing it out the window of your car as you drive down the street, or putting into a balloon and letting it sail away doesn't count. Those things don't count because taking those kinds of actions mean that, in the end, it's possible that somebody else will end up with that dollar bill. And the idea of this exercise isn't to pass money on to somebody else. The idea is to destroy the paper and ink that make up the dollar bill and make that bill unusable.

Resist the temptation to reconcile the idea that throwing a dollar bill away is the same thing as destroying it. It isn't the same thing, and taking that approach won't bring you the intended results of this exercise.

We're aware that this idea may border on blasphemy for some people. The idea of destroying a dollar bill is contrary to what we were taught, especially if our parents, grandparents, or great-grandparents were "depression kids" who often may not have had enough to eat, or decent clothes to wear in the 1930's. And, it may be a painful experience for some, more than just wasteful, destructive, or even considered illegal.

But, as we said at the beginning of this chapter, this is a book about prosperity, and we want you to get *it*. And in order for you to get it, you have to be comfortable about money…that stuff that's made up of ink and paper and has all that easily explained information on it. In order to be comfortable with money, you need to know that it doesn't have a hold over you, and that it doesn't control your life. Getting rid of one simple little dollar bill proves that to yourself. So, get rid of it.

Once you've taken the bold step of confirming the money doesn't control you, but that you do, in fact, have control over it, you can move on to achieving total prosperity in your life. As we like to say, you can have prosperity, and live it.

In addition to the money being the root of all evil issue, there are other things we may have picked up through our lifetime that colors our judgments about money. One of these is the familiar saying that "money doesn't buy happiness." This statement is usually trotted out in an attempt to make people feel better about the fact that somebody else has more money than they do. When a wealthy person or family is dealing with a tragedy that becomes news, this is the statement that the person sitting at the bar mouths before taking another sip of beer.

And the philosophy, unfortunately, is dumped on us by the media in different ways, even in the form "entertainment" on television and in the movies.

One example of this is a T.V. series that was popular in the 1970's. In "Dallas" the Ewing's had all the money they needed. There were a wealthy Texas oil family, living on an expansive ranch, driving expensive cars, and carrying an array of credit cards that allowed them to travel and shop at the best stores. They had a staff to take care of things around the ranch, clean their house, and serve their meals. They had everything money could buy. They also drank too much, were often hung over and miserable, fought amongst each other about everything under the sun, tried to find happiness through extramarital affairs, and in general, came off as being totally pissed off most of the time.

And much of America loved it.

When J.R. and Susan threw their whiskey glasses at each other, the viewing audience knew that "money doesn't buy happiness." When Bobby and J.R. wanted to strangle each other, it showed that "money doesn't buy happiness." When a child only wanted the approval of a parent and instead was only browbeaten again, it was clear that "money doesn't buy happiness."

The long list of television shows, movies and novels that portray characters that have a great deal of money but are miserable most of the time owe their popularity to the idea that "money doesn't buy happiness." Many people read the book or watch the show or movie so they'll feel better about their economic station in life. "Well," they think, ""I may not be rich, but at least I don't (whatever mistake it is that the wealthy character is making at the moment) have *that* in my life."

And so it goes, perpetuating the idea that "money doesn't buy happiness."

This is one example of dealing with two thought patterns that are diametrically opposed to each other, creating stress and confusion for those who desire to achieve prosperity in their lives. First, someone wants to be prosperous and have all the money they want and need, understanding that it's just a method of exchange (the new information we just presented), and then the "money doesn't buy happiness" idea (the established belief and opinion) creeps into their consciousness. And whenever this happens, there has to be some reconciliation of the two ideas or bits of information in order to be able to embrace the new information and move on. In the case of the "money doesn't buy happiness" syndrome, for example, a realistic look at a revised idea can solve the situation.

How about this idea? "Money doesn't buy happiness, but the lack of money may buy you unhappiness and misery."

Think about it. If you had to get across town from point A to point B, and you had no money whatsoever in your pocket, your only option would be to walk. But, if you had the price of bus fare, your trip would be less strenuous and time consuming. You could make your way to a bus stop, wait for the right bus to come along, and take it so you can get directly to, or at least close to your destination. Or, if you had a few dollars more, you wouldn't have to wait for a bus. With a higher level of resources at hand, you could take a cab, which means that you would be riding along in private after being picked up at Point A, then being dropped off at Point B.

And, with an even higher level of resources at your disposal, there is a fourth way to make the trip. That is, of course, to use your own vehicle. The vehicle you bought, or are buying while spending whatever you have to spend in order to maintain, insure and operate it. And with a continuing rise in resources, there is a fifth way to reach your destination. You could simply tell your chauffeur where you want to go and relax in the back seat while you're driven there.

What is the fundamental difference between the five options? A different level of resources at hand…more or less money.

Whether or not any of the options we described is unhappy or miserable is up to you. Perhaps walking is exactly what you want to do because you decided you wanted to walk for whatever reason. It could be exercise, wanting to take in the sights as you walk along, or whatever. And, what about taking the bus? Perhaps you've decided that you enjoy taking public transportation because you're doing your part to keep the environment clean. Taking a cab? Maybe you never learned to drive, or don't want to. If so, taking a cab is something you would enjoy, not something that would bring you misery and unhappiness. And, if you're driving your own car or making the trip in a chauffeured vehicle, you're doing so because that's what you decided to do and had the resources at hand to allow you to make that choice.

Now, if you're walking and you're angry about the fact that you don't have bus fare, that's misery and unhappiness. If you're riding the bus and you don't like it, wishing all the time you're riding on the bus that you could afford to take a cab, that's misery and unhappiness. If you're in a cab and you would prefer to be in your own vehicle, that's misery and unhappiness. And, if you're driving in your own car, while all the time wanting to be in a situation where you could be driven from Point A to Point B while you relax or do something else you consider to be more productive, even that could be misery and unhappiness.

Money could buy you the happiness of getting across town in the fashion you prefer, or the lack of money could cause you to be miserable and unhappy if you felt you were being forced to walk, take the bus or a cab, or drive your own car when you would rather be chauffeured to your destination. Or, yes, you could be staring unhappily out the window of your limo, not really seeing anything because you were troubled about something other than money, such as a relationship issue. It's up to you. Money can only buy happiness if you allow it to do so, and the lack of money can only be responsible for misery and unhappiness if you allow that situation to manifest itself. Like we said, it's up to you.

One way for you to understand where you are about money and/or the lack or abundance of it, is to consider what your emotion would be if you saw the following bumper sticker on the back of a car.

'All I want is a chance to prove that money can't buy me happiness.'

How would that strike you? Would you see it as a light-hearted and humorous or would it bring up some old negative thoughts about money and make you shake your head and utter, "tell me about it buddy'? If it's the latter, then we would encourage you to consider just how destructive that kind of thinking is for you.

And what about that 'love of money being the root of all evil' shtick that many people seem to like to hold onto? On that, we can take a simple and direct approach with one word: Balance.

Sure, we need money in today's society in order to bring home the bacon and buy other things we want and need. But we also, as human beings, need something else. We need to achieve intrinsic satisfaction from any work that we do. That means that we want to know that we have made a contribution to society in some way, otherwise, we're left with a hollow feeling about ourselves and the life we live. We need to achieve balance.

Career, family, relationships with others outside our family, and our relationship with whatever spirituality (not necessarily religion) means to us, are all parts of achieving balance. It just makes sense that focusing or obsessing on one thing and one thing only isn't a healthy proposition for us as a human being. We're just too complex to be one-dimensional, which means that the achievement of balance in all things is of paramount importance to us.

But, the fact is, in our society, some of the baggage and baloney that swirls around us as children (and subsequently as adults) gets in the way of our achievement of balance and allowing money to buy us happiness. For example, children learn early in life that the subject of money and how much of it one has is a subject that is almost as taboo as sex. An innocent five-year-old asking the question "How much money do you make?" in a room full of adults can bring all conversation to a screeching halt. Mom and Dad would be shocked and horrified that their child would put Uncle Dave in such an embarrassing situation and it wouldn't take long after the pin-drop silence for parental reaction to kick in.

Many of us learned early that asking someone how much money they have (which, in our society, is actually asking someone how much money they *don't* have) is something you just don't do. Most parents, and everyone else around a child, are more tolerant of innocent inquiries about why somebody is in a wheelchair or missing a limb than about asking money questions, deciding that natural, innocent curiosity is OK on those other issues. But asking about money to try and understand what it's all about...well that is a completely different story.

Growing up, we didn't understand why this was so. Later in life, though, we figured out that the amount of money one had was the yardstick by which their success was measured. And for many, this yardstick becomes the measurement of how much of a success they're *not*, which can lead to two things that simply cannot be in our lives if we are to have, and live, prosperity. One is obsessing about money (the root of all evil idea) and, the second is letting a preoccupation about money get in the way of enjoying all the other things in our lives (the balance idea) that makes us prosperous.

Watching your five-year-old daughter move as gracefully as possible across the stage in a fall dance recital can make you feel prosperous....if you're not obsessing or out of balance about money. Cheering from the stands as your fifteen-year-old son scores a touchdown or kicks the winning goal can make you feel prosperous....if you're not obsessing or out of balance about money. Watching the networking project you've worked on for weeks come to life can make you feel prosperous....if you're not obsessing or out of balance about money. Accepting the quarterly sales award while a roomful of your colleagues applaud your achievement can make you feel prosperous....if you're not obsessing and out of balance about money. And the list goes on.

So, how do you get there? How do you not obsess about or not be out of balance about money when you feel like your credit card debt, gasoline prices, taxes, food prices, and everything, it seems, except your income, is going up? Well, there is no cookie-cutter, fits-all solution that works for everybody in exactly the same way, but there are some simple steps to get you started on your way.

One of the necessary things is something we've already talked about, understanding on a fundamental level what money really is; paper and ink and a tool that's used for exchange purposes. It's not a mysterious, elusive thing with a lot of strange symbols that hide secrets from only the select few who are somehow lucky enough to be part of the in crowd. And, another thing to understand is that comparing is out.

Wasting time considering how much money your brother, sister, cousin, neighbor, Bill Gates, Abdul Fayed, Tiger Woods, or anybody else has, is just that…a waste of time. Wasting time comparing takes away from time that should be spent figuring out how to either spend less or make more. Which brings us to the question, if you decide not to spend less, but make more, how do you do that?

"MONEY DOESN'T BUY HAPPINESS, BUT THE LACK OF MONEY MAY BUY YOU UNHAPPINESS AND MISERY."

The complete answer to that question is what this first segment of this book, and those that follow, are about. However, since money is, as we said, an important part about prosperity, we'll address a simple issue about money that will start you down the path to making more of it, if that's what you desire. And that simple issue is, consider the baggage that much of our society is carrying around about money.

How did you hear from your parents, grandparents, or whoever it was that was trying to teach you the value of money? Was it, "Money doesn't grow on trees, you know!" when you asked for something?

By whatever process this lack and limitation philosophy may have been handed down to you, replace it with another philosophy. A philosophy that says lack and limitation just ain't where it's at for prosperous people. A philosophy that says although you understand that money doesn't, in fact, grow on trees, there is plenty of it available out there. All you have to do is figure out what you need to do in order to have more of that available money come into your life.

Consider this: All the money you want or need is now in somebody else's pocket, checking account, savings account, or is part of their buying power in the form of credit. That's true for individuals and businesses alike. In order for any of that money to come to you, you need to figure out what you can provide that is of value to somebody else, something that will make them willing to exchange some of the money that's in their "pocket". It could be a product or service that you provide independently. It could be that you've decided to enter into an employment agreement with a small or large business.

It doesn't matter what you decide, but decide, and understand this fundamental principle: You've got to put it in before you get it out in order to be part of the exchange process.

When we provide a product or our expertise, we wind up with money from that exchange. Then, we exchange the money we got for whatever we provided for one of two things…either another person's time or expertise, or for a product that they or their company provides.

Another element of the lack and limitation idea is rooted in a different place, fostered and supported by myths. The most common of these myths is that in order to reach a certain level of wealth, a person has to be ruthless, uncaring, selfish, and willing to step on anybody and everybody on their way to the top.

Maybe you've been told that the reason the Kennedy family has all the money they have is because Papa Kennedy made a bunch of money as a bootlegger, and that he would probably have been willing to throw an immigrant or two overboard if that's what took to keep the authorities from intercepting his liquor shipments. Maybe somebody told you that Henry

Ford had a habit of placing a large order with a company, then canceling at the last minute so he could buy the now-strapped company cheap. Maybe you were told that while history treats Thomas Edison as a mild-mannered inventor whose experiments and inventions benefited mankind, he actually stole his success from Nikola Tesla, or others.

Or, maybe you've never heard any of these specific stories before. Maybe the ones you heard were different, but they had the same point to them as the ones we've presented. The idea behind the stories (whether they had a grain of truth to them or not) was to convey and perpetuate the myth that in order to get rich, one has to be dishonest, ruthless, or some combination of the two. Nothing could be further from the truth. The idea of money being nothing more than a medium of exchange is one of the elements of the foundation of a wealthy person's understanding of how the world works, not ruthlessness or dishonesty.

Is it possible that there are examples to the contrary out there? Is it possible that somebody has made a lot of money through dishonest acts? Of course somebody has, but there are two things to understand about them. First, they're in the minority, and second, whatever wealth they managed to garner often doesn't last.

Drug dealers may make a boatload of money while they're engaged in an illegal activity, but they are often a statistic long before they would be eligible for membership in AARP. A dictator may amass unimaginable wealth, but only because many people live in miserable conditions. These are the kinds of situations that are often the focus of attention, so the myth persists.

And while we're on the subject of focusing attention on the minority, and how it often presents a lopsided picture of the facts, here are some statistics about self-made millionaires and where they come from:

74%: Start and operate their own business.

10%: Hold senior level executive positions in large corporations.

10%: Are doctors or lawyers.

5%: Are in sales.

Now, if you're doing the simple math here, what you'll see is that the figures we've presented add up to 99%. And, by and large, most of these people are not the focus of media attention. Most often, the news is about people in show business, professional sports, people who invent something or make a bundle in the stock market, or it's about people who win the lottery. And it's true that entertainers, investors and lottery winners become millionaires. It's also true that all these categories of people together make up one-percent of all self-made millionaires.

And now that we've explored the myths and presented the facts on self-made millionaires, we'll take a look at another common money baggage issue, related to the idea of inherited wealth. The way this idea is often expressed is through statements like "the rich get richer while the poor get poorer" or "in order to make a lot of money, you have to have a lot of money in the first place."

It's even possible that some people feel cheated or angry about the fact that while others inherit wealth, they won't. And it looks, from their perspective that large numbers of people either have, or stand to inherit lots of money. Well, here's a statistic on that issue. A 1997 survey showed that the percentage of households in the United States with a net worth of more than a million dollars…wealth that could be passed on to the next generation…was six-percent. This simply meant that ninety-four percent of the people in the United States weren't in a position to inherit a million dollars in 1997.

Even with the advent of the dot.com boom (and bust in some cases) and other societal and business factors since that survey, the percentage point rise was minimal. According to a later CNN survey, seven-percent (leaving 93% instead of 94% left) of American households had a net worth of over a million dollars, which was related to the rise in real estate values.

Obviously, these percentages have likely changed again since the financial crisis that resulted in widespread foreclosures on home mortgages. And you likely know somebody who has lost their job and their home, or gone through a short sale. But, look around and notice something else. There are also a lot of people who haven't lost their jobs, or they adjusted when necessary, finding income through channels that were not even thought of ten years ago.

Our point in presenting the statistics we mentioned and citing the differences between people who are and are not negatively affected by what's going on around them is simply to illustrate the idea that we presented earlier; that much of our society is either carrying around a lot of baggage about money, or focusing on stories that may or may not be true about certain people who have made a lot of money. Both of these thought processes are based in a philosophy of lack and limitation, which is the exact opposite of having a prosperity consciousness. Here are two scenarios for you to consider about money and having a prosperity consciousness:

Scenario #1: You have always loved old cars. You're driving along one day and you notice a nearly-restored, primer-painted 1938 Chevrolet parked near a body shop. The sign on the windshield says the car is for sale for $4,000. You are presently in a money situation that isn't, and hasn't for a long time, been prosperous. You barely have enough money in your checking account to get you through to the next payday. How do you feel about your love of old cars at this moment?

Scenario #2: You have always loved old cars. You're driving along one day and you notice a nearly-restored, primer-painted 1938 Chevrolet parked near a body shop. The sign on the windshield says the car is for sale for $4,000. You have, through whatever activities have worked for you, approximately $10,000 in the bank, and you are having no trouble paying all your monthly bills. You take an extended look at the car, knowing that you could, if you wanted to, pull over and buy it.

You decide that you would prefer not to use the resources you have available to you at the moment to buy the car because it would leave you less money than you would like to have on hand in the bank. How do you feel about your love of old cars at the moment?

The point of presenting these two scenarios was to illustrate the concept of knowing you are in control of your life, versus the feeling that you are not. Knowing you are in control allows you to experience prosperity, while on the other hand, believing you're not in control, prevents you from knowing, feeling, and understanding prosperity.

One more concept we want to mention relative to feeling you are in control of your life, is in regard to a familiar phrase…The All-Mighty Dollar. People you meet may be inclined to use this phrase when they talk about money, and when they do, the thought and opinion behind their use of the phrase is not pleasant or positive.

Recently, we visited with somebody who, in the course of our conversation about the two most famous Philly Cheese Steak Sandwich restaurants in Philadelphia, Pat's and Geno's, which are located across the street from each other, used this term. In his opinion, one of the restaurants we were discussing was focused on making the best sandwich possible, while the other was "more interested in the All-Mighty Dollar"……as though making money while at the same time focusing on how to make the best sandwich possible was somehow an unsavory idea.

While others present simply nodded their heads in agreement (or, at the very least, didn't really notice what he said, and the philosophy behind it), our take on the situation was that we were presented with yet another opportunity to ignore a negative opinion about money, something that you can be sure that you will encounter from time to time.

(By the way, we recently went to Philadelphia to tour the city and conduct our own Philly Cheesesteak taste test. It was a great fun, and we highly recommend spending some time there.)

Before you jump to the conclusion that we're being radical about this subject, or way too sensitive about what some people say in our presence about money, please consider an idea that we will re-visit as we go along through this book: That things that seem minor, or even barely noticeable, can affect your prosperity consciousness without your even being aware of those things. And while the first segment of this book is largely about money, this entire book is not only about money. It's about achieving total prosperity in your life, and that requires making prosperity an integral part of your values and belief system.

A belief system that, unfortunately, will not be shared by some people you meet, with their opinion that life is a zero sum game… meaning that there's only just so much to go around, and if somebody has a lot of prosperity, that means that somebody else is going to be cheated out of experiencing some prosperity… but that is simply not the truth (we'll tell you why as we go along). So you simply have to be aware that it's part of life that negative influences about money and a prosperity consciousness are out there, and you have to be aware of being exposed to them so you can consciously ignore them.

At the beginning of this chapter, we said that what we wanted was for you to get it about prosperity, about having prosperity and living prosperity…about developing a prosperity consciousness. And now that the topic of money is out of the way, allowing you to work toward getting *it*, we can move on to our next subject, which is…..

NOTES:

_____

_____

_____

_____

_____

_____

_____

SEGMENT TWO

DESIRE: THE STARTING POINT FOR EVERYTHING

SEGMENT TWO:
DESIRE: THE STARTING POINT FOR EVERYTHING

Yes, desire is the starting point for everything. Whatever we have accomplished as a society started as a desire to provide something for society. A system to provide medical care for indigent people started as a desire to do so. A system to help underwrite the cost of daycare for low-income families started out as a desire to provide that service. Our laws, law-enforcement, and justice system all came about as a result of the desire to create such a system.

And, desire is the starting point for all the things we do as individuals. People who produce and direct movies do so because they have a desire to communicate and entertain others through the production and direction of movies. People who watch movies do so because they have a desire to be entertained. People who write books do so because they have a desire to communicate with others through the process of writing books. People who read books do so because they have a desire to be either educated or entertained.

People become teachers because they have a desire to teach others. People become doctors because they have a desire to provide medical care to others. People start businesses because they have a desire to provide a product or service to others through a business of their own. People become ministers, priests or rabbis because they want to serve the spiritual needs of others.

Desire is it. Desire is why we do what we do as a society and why we do what we do as an individual. We do it because we want to do it, because we have a desire to do it. And why do we have a desire to do things?

Because, as a human being, we have within us an innate desire to succeed.

We want to be a success to ourselves and to others. We want to feel successful and achieve inner satisfaction, and we want to be a success in the eyes of society, our family…parents, siblings, children, spouses…we want to be a success in the eyes of those we work with on a daily basis, or those we meet only once in our lifetime. We have a desire to succeed.

That's what desire is. And, what desire is not is a wish.

If someone says "I wish I had a million dollars," then that's all they have is a wish. But, if someone decides that they have a burning desire for a million dollars, then they'll find a way to fulfill that desire.

If someone says, "I wish I didn't have to work for somebody else. I wish I had my own business," they will likely spend a lot of time wishing, but not a lot of time doing. Having a *desire* to own a business, though, leads a person to take what available time they have after their day of working for someone else and start building toward achieving what they desire.

Having a wish to own a business usually leads a person to wish about while they're dealing with some difficulty at work…."I wish I didn't have to put up with this crap every day."

Having a wish to own a business usually leads to thinking about it while on the way home from work in the evening…."I wish I didn't have to fight this darn traffic all the time"

Having a wish to own a business usually leads a person to wish for that while they're thumbing through a magazine or zoned out in front of the T.V. after dinner. Having a wish to own a business usually leads a person to wish for that while they're relaxing during the weekend. These are the things that wishing to own a business usually lead a person to do.

Having a desire to own a business, though, leads a person to do things differently.

Having a desire to own a business will lead a person to make the best use of their time while they're stuck in traffic…."I'm going to listen to chapter two of that audio book on CD while I'm driving into work today," and they don't let excuses get in their way. For example, if a person with a desire rather than a wish wants to listen to an audio book, but they don't have the resources at the moment to purchase it, they make a trip to the library. There is a wealth of information available there, and all it takes is a library card.

Having a desire to own a business usually leads a person to look at the challenges they deal with at work on a daily basis from a learning perspective, such as…."Well, now I know what kind of unworkable system I'll never put in place when I have my own business."

Having a desire to own a business leads a person to invest some of their weekend relaxing time in a different way from someone who is only wishing. They invest some of their time taking a class or reading a book on bookkeeping, or marketing, or advertising. Or they learn how to write a business plan, sell successfully, or whatever it is they need to know in order to start and operate the business they desire. That's the difference between a wish and a desire.

It's simply that a wish often causes a person to spend their time in a passive mode, even feeling beaten up by their wish. If a person wishes they owned a business, but they believe they can't even begin to get it off the ground because they 'don't have the capital' to get it started, then they'll spend their time depressively, wishing. With a burning desire as motivation, though, a person will keep taking some kind of action until they find a way to get their hands on the money they need to get started. If necessary, they'll save the money they need by sacrificing in ways that wishers would never consider. They'll borrow it from others if they have to, taking the risk on their belief that they can succeed.

A person with an absolutely burning desire won't allow obstacles to prevent them from achieving that desire. A person with a desire will find a way to fulfill that desire. A person with a wish will keep on wishing.

Although we've used the example of owning a business in our discussion on the difference between wishing and desiring, we want to point out that the concept isn't limited to owning a business when considering the idea of total prosperity.

"Desire is it. Desire is why we do what we do as a society and why we do what we do as an individual."

If you wish for a relationship, that's one thing...desiring it and taking action is another. Wishing for a promotion at work is one thing...desiring it and learning what you need to learn or doing what you need to do to put yourself in line for that promotion is another.

Wishing you had a new living room sofa is one thing...finding a way to buy, negotiate for, trade for, or do whatever you need to do in order to get that sofa is another. If simply does not matter whether it's professional, personal, monetary, spiritual, or whatever label you want to put on it; having a desire leads to having that desire fulfilled and living out your desire, while wishing leads to...more wishing.

There's no doubt that the germ of desire itself is a wish, hope or dream. We all need wish in the beginning, and hope and dream. But from that germ of an idea or thought, something inside of us has to turn that dream, hope or wish into a burning desire. A hope can be fulfilled, a dream can be realized, and a wish can come true through desire. It's *desire* that gives you the energy you need to meet a challenge and get through it so you can reach your goal of having what you want to have, be what you want to be or do what you want to do.

Desire is the mental fuel that you need to "keep on keepin' on" when it seems as though anything that can go wrong, does, because you've made the wrong choice at the wrong time. If your wish, hope, or dream hasn't grown into a desire, you'll find yourself running on empty in a hurry while you're meeting the day-to-day things that can get in the way of having what you want. If you have a true desire, you have the capacity to reach down deep when you need to and make new choices or better decisions, turning wrongs into rights, and mistakes into learning experiences. Desire is part of *it*...*it* being what we want you to get about having and living a prosperous life.

You can prove to yourself the fact that desire is the starting point of success. Whether you're fifteen or fifty, think back to a point in your life experience where you decided you really wanted something. It could be something you think of as insignificant now, but at the time it was a major undertaking for you. Whatever it was, however much effort it took, or whatever it took moneywise, workwise or whateverwise, you got it or did it.

And the reason you were able to succeed was because even though it started out as a wish, hope or dream, you made the decision at some point to turn what you wished, dreamed or hoped for into a desire. And when you made that decision, you either consciously or unconsciously used a formula to turn your desire into a reality.

The formula isn't complicated, it doesn't take a Herculean effort to use, nor does it take years of education to understand. Here are the simple steps that made up the formula you used:

1. You decided exactly what it was that you wanted. You weren't vague about it. It was a focused, measureable, definite decision about something.
2. You determined what it was that you had to give in exchange for what you wanted, and then you committed to finding a way to do that, no matter how difficult it would be.
3. You set a deadline for getting what you wanted.
4. You decided on, then stuck with (or intelligently modified if necessary) a step-by-step plan of what you needed to do.

Those were the steps you took, and they are the steps you can take again to achieve and live prosperously.

Of course, one important element of your success was a factor we mentioned within step four. A specific plan of action is certainly necessary when we want to accomplish anything worthwhile, but it's also necessary that we be open to new information or opportunities we simply couldn't have been aware of when we formulated our plan. Human nature being what it is, this idea isn't always easy to accept. Letting our ego take over can sometimes be seamless, and when that happens, we can operate with blinders on because we're so focused on what we're absolutely certain is the "right" thing to do as we follow our plan.

"A PERSON WITH AN ABSOLUTELY BURNING DESIRE WON'T ALLOW OBSTACLES TO PREVENT THEM FROM ACHIEVING THAT DESIRE. A PERSON WITH A DESIRE WILL FIND A WAY TO FULFILL THAT DESIRE. A PERSON WITH A WISH WILL KEEP ON WISHING."

In Segment One we mentioned that having a prosperity consciousness is a belief system. Sometimes, a person's belief system about what "right" is can get in the way of their developing that belief system and accomplishing the achievement of total prosperity in their life. Often what's "right" or what is the "truth" is not really the truth, but only the truth as one perceives it to be. And, often this perception is not the correct one, often focused on alleged limitations in ability. For example, if someone… anyone, in a position of authority told you what you were or weren't good at when you were a child, that can become a belief.

"You're just not good at math," you might have been told by a teacher, or even a parent who thought it might give you courage to try harder if you knew you needed to develop your math skills.

But often, it doesn't work out that way. What develops is a belief that "I'm just not good at math," and this belief can be held for an entire lifetime if something doesn't come along to precipitate a change in that belief. And, this is where the need to be "right" comes in.

When someone believes that they're not good at something, a thought pattern that is best described as psychological homeostasis is established. The term homeostasis itself defines being in balance, or in harmony. A person is the medical profession, for example, would like all of their patients to achieve homeostasis because it would mean that their circulatory and respiratory systems were working together in harmony, leading to good health. However, the concept of achieving psychological homeostasis is not always the picture of good psychological health. Because of a our inherent human need to be "right" about things, our belief that we're not good at something is responsible for the actual results that we achieve in a given area of expertise or skill.

To put it simply, our subconscious mind works to make sure that whatever we do in the area of that skill or expertise we believe we're not good at, serves to prove that we're right in our belief. If we believe we're not good at math, a math problem will stump us, and we'll be able to say, "See, I told you I wasn't good at math," proving that we are right about our belief, allowing us to achieve psychological homeostasis.

Evidence of people achieving psychological homeostasis with a negative outcome is all around us, but not often evident until somebody points it out to us. Consider the world of professional sports….anyone who follows baseball, football or basketball will likely be able to tell you about at least one "rising star" who crashed and burned long before their time. The athlete who had tremendous potential, and, through hard work and dedication, reached dizzying heights of accomplishment, only to waste it all through the abuse of drugs, and/or alcohol, or some other form of destructive behavior. And there are also many examples of this self-destruction by someone who seemingly "has it all" in the entertainment industry.

Every generation has puzzled over a fabulously talented actor, singer or musician who, it's discovered in the end, was a tortured soul who committed slow or instant suicide (and, whether it was a drug overdose or a car accident, it wasn't an *accident* since there are no *accidents*, only events that take place). And while the specifics may vary from one case to another, looking closely at every situation would show that there was an underlying cause for their misery and eventual downfall….their belief that they didn't deserve all the good fortune that had come upon them, and their need to achieve psychological homeostasis and be "right" about their life experience. An overpowering need to ruin or end either their prosperous life entirely, doing whatever it took to accomplish that unfortunate goal.

At the risk of raising the ire of the entire city of Memphis, Tennessee (and likely legions of other people around the country) we'll consider what happened to one of the world's most famous entertainers,

Elvis. There's no doubt that at a point early in his career, his immense talent was responsible for the meteoric rise of his star. Hit songs, adoring fans, movie deals, and merchandising, along with all the fame and fortune that went along with it, were his.

A young man born into a poor family in Tupelo, Mississippi who rose to a level of recognition and notoriety so immense that you don't even need to use his last name when you speak of him. Everybody knows who you're talking about when you mention only his first name. Those are the facts.

It's also a fact that once he entered the Army and was introduced to drugs, he was hooked from that time forward, and faced a lifetime of chemical ingestion that ranged from drugs that slowed him down to those that got him to speed up. In the face of nothing but fame, fortune, more money that he could ever spend in a lifetime, and a career that he was obviously destined to pursue, bringing entertainment, joy and pleasure to millions of people, his abuse of prescription (and some not-so prescription) drugs never left him, and in the end, he died unhappy, and, even though he was surrounded by people, alone.

No matter what decade you consider, people can remember a sports or entertainment personality who crashed and burned, all the while shaking their heads and wondering why they would destroy themselves when they have so much to live for…live happily and prosperously.

For example, there's the eighteen-year-old who had extraordinary skills in throwing a baseball, and made it to the big leagues before he reached the legal drinking age in his state, then fell into cocaine abuse within a short time after his career got off the ground.

And the young comedian who not only did a great stand-up act, but also wound up starring in his own #1 rated sit-com, who put a pistol to his head and ended his life. His hit show was still on the air the day he died.

And it's not just athletes or entertainers who, after being thrust into a limelight that they're not prepared for, wind up dying young or living a life of misery. It happens in business professions, the trades, health care, education, or any other profession or craft you consider. It also happens in relationships…somebody not believing that they deserve some one, and then finding some way to drive them away. Psychological homeostasis is a powerful element of the human journey through life, and unfortunately, it often winds up in a negative result. But, it doesn't have to be that way.

In the same way that a person can harbor the belief that they "don't deserve" something or someone, they can also *decide* that they *do* deserve the good things in life. (Note the emphasis in that sentence.) And, once they decide that's the "truth" about their self, then that's how they'll achieve psychological homeostasis….in a positive way rather than a negative one.

In addition to the psychological homeostasis approach to having and living prosperity, an important element of prosperous thinking is the understanding that we are always surrounded by an abundance of resources. And thinking of these resources through any sort of limited perspective, whether we are comfortable admitting it or not, can limit our success. A positive approach to understanding the concept of abundance could be as simple as being able to recognize that in order to accomplish anything worthwhile, we need to decide on a plan, put it down on paper, and be open to the idea that a key element of that plan may be that you'll shift gears or make a slight adjustment in another direction when necessary.

Consider this idea from the simple perspective of getting on a jet in New York for a flight to Los Angeles. When the aircraft takes off, a flight plan identifying the destination is obviously in place. However, during the flight, the pilot will likely make minor adjustments in order to make sure that landing takes place in exactly the correct spot more than 2,000 miles away, and on schedule.

To help you re-trace the steps you took to success and achievement in the past, and show you how you can use them in mapping out a prosperous future, we'll move on to our next segment. Once you understand that desire is the starting point of all success, that next step you need to take is.....

NOTES:

_____

_____

_____

_____

_____

_____

SEGMENT THREE

DECIDING WHAT YOU WANT....
YOU HAVE TO DO IT

SEGMENT THREE
DECIDING WHAT YOU WANT....
YOU HAVE TO DO IT

We believe that everyone knows instinctively that enjoying freedom and living prosperously is their birthright. It's just that it sometimes takes an effort on our part to wake up and "remember" that truth. It's easy to dismiss this idea as too much of a pie-in-the-sky attitude, but it is just that...the truth.

Walk into a paint store with a specific color in mind, and no matter what it is, you'll be able to walk out with a gallon of exactly what you want. When you pick the color off a chart, somebody, anybody who has taken the time to become familiar with the particular system used at that paint store, can consult an instruction sheet, then follow specific instructions to add a specific amount of various tints to a can of white base paint, with the end result being exactly what you decided you wanted in a color. And this idea doesn't end there.

In this digital age, you don't have to pick a color just from a chart. With a swatch of material or pillow from the furniture in the room, your exact color can be scanned and fed into a computer system that directs the mixing of the various tints into the white base that becomes a gallon of exactly what you decided you wanted.

The key here is that you decided exactly what color you wanted, then found a way...as system, actually...to get what you wanted. Achieving and living a prosperous life works the same way. First, a specific decision is reached. Nothing is vague or left to chance as far as the goal. Then, a system is employed to take whatever specific actions are necessary to bring what started out as nothing more than a desire to fruition....the achievement of specific goals.

It's been said that a goal is really nothing more than a dream with a deadline, and we agree. People can dream all day long about what they want in their life, but until they make a decision about what they want, then put into action a specific plan to have what it is they're dreaming about, a dream will still be just a dream, and they'll have the same dream tomorrow, and the next day, and the next....

One way to understand the approach to effective goal-setting is to consider the simple to-do list. Do you ever use one? Perhaps when you are faced with a busy day that involves getting a list of things done in order to make sure that the kids have what they need for school, that things will go smoothly at your job, and the upcoming visit of your out-of-town family member will be a pleasant visit? If so, you may have employed a to-do list to keep you on track and get all the necessary tasks you need to get accomplished in order to juggle all the situations you're dealing with at the moment and have them work out the way you want....and there it is....*deciding what you want*. As we said, you've got to do it.

A to-do list is not an ultimate goals list, but it is similar, and it always helps people get things done. In the 1930's, the president of U.S. Steel called in a consultant and asked for advice on how top management in the company could get more tasks accomplished on any given day. The advice was simple: "Have everybody make a simple list of the things they need to get done in a day, listing them in their order of importance. Make sure they get the first task accomplished before moving on to the next item on their list."

The top executive not only took the consultant's advice and implemented the simple procedure, he wrote a check for $25,000 (remember, this is the 1930's) after the consultant said that he would wait for his client to determine what the idea was worth before deciding how much to pay for the advice. What was the company president's reason for writing such a large check for such a simple idea? He considered it responsible for amazing growth and success within his company.

To-do lists work because they share a similar trait to a goals list....they are in writing. Sure, to-do lists are made up of sometimes mundane tasks that need to be accomplished, but they can also contain a task that is important and related to a goal. Here are some of the items on a recent to-do list of ours:

1. Transfer deed for Downing Street property.
2. Get oil changed on the Gold Wing.
3. Assemble new recumbent exercise bike.

The first item on the list, while it is a task, is related to a long-term goal we are working on; buying residential properties and holding them for a term that allows us to re-sell them for profit when the housing market improves. Yes, it's a task, but it's also part of a goal.

Beyond your daily to-do lists, you can create a goals list of not just the things you need to do in order to stay organized and, in the process, feel as though you're in control of your life…that's an important issue related to the goal setting process…writing down everything you would like to have, do, or be in the next 30 days, 1 year, or, if you're considering a long-range goal, in 5 years. Providing you're taking a *realistic* approach to accomplishing something….deciding you want to be a brain surgeon by the end of next month, and not having yet set foot into medical school is not being realistic…writing it down is a key to achieving it.

As an example, let's say you decided that in a year's time, you want to own your own home. You're renting at the moment, and you've *decided* (note, another key term) that you're going to be a homeowner, and you've decided that it's realistic that you'll be able to achieve that goal at the end of a 12-month time frame. If you decided this on December 12th of this year, then you're deadline date for achievement of your goal would be December 12th the following year. **Remember, a goal is a dream with a deadline.**

When you first put a goal such as this down on paper, you might have a hundred questions running through your mind…."How will I come up with the down payment when I'm barely able to afford the rent, utilities and the rest of my monthly bills?" or "Will I be able to afford the monthly mortgage payment?" or even, "What section of town do I want to live in?"

That's OK. Expect to have questions at the outset of achieving a major life goal such as buying a house. When effectively using the goal-setting process of writing things down, you have to get started with not only a realistic idea, but with faith that you can accomplish your goal.

"It's impossible to steal second base if you keep one foot on first."

Anonymous

But, it's not pie-in-the-sky faith we want you to have. It's faith that you'll find a way to accomplish what you set out do because of the way your Reticular Activating System functions. Perhaps you've never heard of a *Reticular Activating System (RAS for short)*. Everybody has one. RAS is a part of the human condition, and it is continually functioning in your behalf, whether you know it or not.

The simple way to understand RAS is to define the first segment of the term…reticular, which is a word with Latin roots meaning 'net' or 'net-like'. We like to refer to RAS as a 'thought net'. The basic function of your 'thought net' is to keep you on track to achieve what you set out to do, and it does that by acting as a filter of sorts, which allows things that are not important to the goal that is on your mind to be 'caught' in your 'thought net' while allowing the things that are not important to you to pass through the openings in your net, and be quickly dismissed by your consciousness, not allowing them to clutter your mind and thereby prevent you from achieving your goal.

And the bottom line in getting your RAS to work (yep, there's a bit of pun in that sentence if you want to read it into it) is to *write down* your goal. Writing it down first makes it real to you. You may not be 100% comfortable with how this makes you feel the first time you get hit with the emotion that accompanies the action, but keep at it. You'll get used to it. You won't necessarily stop being just a little amazed by the process when you look back on the moment you wrote something down and discovered that in the time frame you set that it works…again! But you'll get used to working with the process and letting it work for you. So *write it down*.

"BEYOND YOUR DAILY TO-DO LISTS, YOU CAN CREATE A GOALS LIST OF NOT JUST THE THINGS YOU NEED TO DO IN ORDER TO STAY ORGANIZED AND, IN THE PROCESS, FEEL AS THOUGH YOU'RE IN CONTROL OF YOUR LIFE…"

Once you write it down, not only does RAS begin to do its work, you now have a method of keeping yourself reminded about your specific goal when you review your list as often as you find it necessary to keep you motivated. But that's not the real magic of RAS. Remember what we said about the "R" is RAS, it means that your mind has a segment that acts like a net, and a net is designed to catch some things while letting some other things go through.

Things that your net catches are the resources and specific things that are important to you, and necessary for you to know about in order to achieve your selected goal. Without deciding on your specific goal and writing it down, those resources and things are there all around you, you just don't see them until your mind is focused on achieving a specific goal. Then you can suddenly "see" those necessary resources and things. Here are two situations we experienced that will help you to understand the concept of RAS....

At one point in time, we decided we needed a new car, and in our search came upon a model we weren't familiar with at all: A Dodge Spirit. It was the car we quickly and easily decided to purchase even though we hadn't heard of it before, a four-door model in a nice medium blue. On the way home from the dealership, you can guess what we saw out there as part of the traffic: Dodge Spirits....lot's of them, and even one in a medium blue, just like the one we bought. Did those Dodge Spirits just magically decide to appear? No, there were always there, we just didn't notice them. And why did we notice them now? Because suddenly, since we had invested some of our money in one, they became important to us, and RAS set to work allowing us to "see" them.

The second situation also involves a car purchase, but this time around, one that was familiar to us. Since our work has, and still does, involve travel either by plane or via automobile, we needed another new vehicle. Acting on the recommendation of friends, we took a close look at a Chevrolet Suburban because it was one choice that we thought might fit our needs. After all, these friends had owned a few of them over the years and were always happy with them. And, by the way, we certainly knew about the Chevrolet Suburban, having ridden in them before, and, via General Motors' marketing efforts, seen T.V. commercials and read dealer ads that featured the Suburban.

But…when we bought one for the first time….you guessed it… we noticed there were a lot more of them than we had ever seen before. Of course, just like the Dodge Spirits, they were always there, moving along through traffic with us, we just didn't notice them until they became more important to us. And, to put it in simple and direct terms, once you write down a goal you want to accomplish, it becomes important and brought to the forefront of your mind, which means that your RAS gets to work (hmmm…there's the pun again) and the resources that were always around you, but unnoticed by you, are suddenly in your consciousness, allowing you the opportunity to use those resources to accomplish your goal.

If you need an increase in income in order to save your down payment and cover the closing costs involved in your home purchase, RAS will help you recognize opportunities that are open to you, and you'll be able to focus your energy on working with those "new-found" opportunities and raise the extra capital you need for your home purchase.

While it's impossible to say exactly what those opportunities will be, whether it's an extra part-time job or a hobby that you'll turn into a part-time business that brings you the extra money you need to save every month for 12 months in order to achieve your goal, RAS will go to work because the thing you want is important in your mind. And it's important in your mind because it's down on paper, making it more real for you than a casually mentioned wish or dream.

By the way, you might be wondering what kind of system you can use to keep track of your daily to-do lists, weekly, monthly, or annual goals. Are we recommending that you get into using one of the organizing systems such as Franklin/Covey or DayTimer that are available? If that's what works for you, OK. But, if you decide to not to use a prepared calendar system and instead employ a simple 98-cent spiral-bound tablet, that's OK too. The only issue that's important about the goal-setting process is getting it down on paper so you can consult it as necessary through the day, week, month or year.

Successful people have employed just about any written method you can imagine, from Post-It notes stuck to the corner of a monitor so it can be noticed every morning when they move their mouse to wake up their computer, to a system with weekly or monthly multi-colored dividers and letter codes identifying the importance level of the items on their goal list. It's up to you.

It's up to you because the specific system you employ is only a tool you'll use to have and live prosperity in your life. The element that motivates you to employ the tools that suit you best in goal-setting and achievement is your beliefs, habits, attitude, and approach to life, and understanding how your arrived at your beliefs, habits, attitude and approach is important because……

NOTES:

SEGMENT FOUR

PROGRAMMING FOR SUCCESS IS A CHOICE….SO IS PROGRAMMING FOR LESS THAN SUCCESS.

SEGMENT FOUR
PROGRAMMING FOR SUCCESS IS A CHOICE....SO IS PROGRAMMING FOR LESS THAN SUCCESS.

Programming....that's an interesting term, isn't it?

For people raised in the 1950's, it meant brainwashing, something that the "Evil Empire" (the USSR, back then) did to secret agents, or even innocent people, in their bid to take over the world. And today, well, programming is a much more innocuous term related to computers and information technology. But, we want you to consider the term "programming" from a perspective other than that of national security or your laptop. Consider it simply from the point of view of how we respond to information we gather as we go through life, and how we decide to use that information.

Here's an example of programming....

Let's say you're a twelve-year-old and, even though you don't know it yet, you have literally an incalculable amount of stuff to learn about life. There you are one day, listening in on a conversation between two guys who, at nearly eighteen, and you (at the moment) are impressed with them because you're sure they know a lot about the world. The subject of the conversation is whether or not one should take a job where the pay is hourly, or on a commission basis.

What you hear:

"Man, none of that commission crap for me. When I go to work I want a guaranteed hourly wage."

"Yeah man, you've got that right."

What you decide:

Getting paid on commission isn't fair....it's risky and you'll likely take home less money than you would if you were getting paid by the hour…it's a method that people who own businesses use to take advantage of people who work for them….etc….etc, depending on what else you might have heard before, or will hear in the future, from other "Authorities-At-The-Moment", such as parents, teachers, older siblings, etc….

In short, negative programming about the subject of working on commission….

Fast forward a half-a-dozen years or so, and you're either looking for your first full-time job after graduating from high school with no plans to go on to college, or a plan to go part time while you work. Or you're looking for a summer or part-time job to help cover school and living expenses. Your scanning research of the classifieds, on-line listings, or whatever, that shows some jobs listing commission as their payment method, and your programming kicks in to help you decide which jobs you'll look into and which jobs you won't even consider.

The problem: Your programming is getting in the way of your potential success, because you're not open to the idea that not all commission jobs (OK, certainly there are *some* that could fit into your programming profile) have an unfair risk factor, take advantage, or limit your income. But there are also reputable businesses that compensate their employees via a variety of incentive programs, and, based on your performance, your earnings could be higher than what you would receive if you worked within an hourly system.

Sure, there's always some risk involved if your profession compensates you via a performance-based system, but again, what is your programming? What have you "decided" about your ability to perform, and earn, from a commission or bonus method of payment?

Hmmm… does it seem as though we're about to launch into a "You can do it!-PMA (Positive Mental Attitude) is everything!-Your attitude affects your altitude!" approach to prosperity that could be construed as a lot of 'hype'? No, we're not into a hollow approach to prosperity, just an honest, down-to-earth approach to understanding a person's approach to, programming of, and consciousness regarding, their abilities and beliefs about themselves. And, the fact of the matter is, taking a positive approach rather than a negative one does have an effect on whether or not you'll succeed at anything you attempt to accomplish.

"THERE ARE NO SECRETS TO SUCCESS. IT IS THE RESULT OF PREPARATION, HARD WORK, AND LEARNING FROM FAILURE."

COLIN POWELL

So let's talk about the difference between optimism and pessimism. And let's not talk about it just from the 'how do you see the glass…half-full or half-empty?' approach, but from the perspective of documented, measurable research that explains how a person's <u>perception of events due to their programming</u>, determines either success or less-than-success in any endeavor.

The underlined segment above says it all: It's about perception. And there is a simplistic approach to explaining a person's perception of events that employs six terms.

They are:

1. Permanent
2. Pervasive
3. Personal
4. Impermanent
5. Isolated
6. Impersonal

You've likely heard the phrase "Mind your Ps and Qs" (which, by the way, depending on the source you prefer to believe means either "mind your pints and quarts", a warning that 17th century pub patrons issued to bartenders keeping track of their tab, or an admonition teachers employ when explaining how to write properly and avoid mixing up the mirror-image letters p and q, or a warning to print shop workers back in the day when they had to sort individual letters back into their proper bins and it would be easy to mix up the two letters), so we'll employ a simple memory aid here and remind you to "mind your P's and I's"

"AND, THE FACT OF THE MATTER IS, TAKING A POSITIVE APPROACH RATHER THAN A NEGATIVE ONE DOES HAVE AN EFFECT ON WHETHER OR NOT YOU'LL SUCCEED AT ANYTHING YOU ATTEMPT TO ACCOMPLISH."

Keep in mind that, like the "Ps and Qs" approach, none of the six words on our list are to be considered either a negative or positive term. Depending on their application to a particular event, they can be either. It's all about events. Events are things that happen to all of us every day, many times a day. And an event is just that, an event, and, depending on your perception of that event, you are either programming for success, or programming for less than success.

Research shows that how a person responds to an event determines whether they are taking an optimistic or pessimistic approach to life. Consider this:

A **positive event** happens, and a person's programming leads them to think:

"OK, it looks like I did my normal thing here," (Personal)... "and, I'm pretty much on my usual track," (Pervasive, meaning present, throughout, everywhere, or spreading widely)..."and I'm sure things will keep on going this way," (Permanent).

What we've just illustrated above is an optimistic approach to a positive event.

And, a **negative event** happens, and a person's programming leads them to think:

"Whoa, that didn't work out," (Impersonal)...."and that's not what normally happens to me," (Isolated)..."and, I'll find a way to turn this around," (Impermanent).

And what we've just illustrated above is, again, an optimistic approach, this time to a negative event.

And now, consider this:

A **positive event** happens, and a person's programming leads them to think:

"Whoa, how did that manage to happen?" (Impersonal)…."that's not what normally happens to me in these situations," (Isolated)…"this is too good to last. It'll all fall apart soon enough" (Impermanent).

And, a **negative event** happens, and a person's programming leads them to think:

"OK, it looks like I did my normal thing here," (Personal)… "my bad luck follows me everywhere I go," (Pervasive, meaning present throughout, everywhere, or spreading widely)…"and that's just the way it is for me," (Permanent).

And, what we've just described above is a pessimistic approach to events.

You get the point. If a person is taking an optimistic approach to the events that occur in life, when a positive event occurs, the programming is from a Personal, Pervasive, and Permanent perspective (Personal…"Yesss… I did it!"… Pervasive…"Chalk up another one for me,"…. Permanent…."What's next"?

And when a negative event occurs, the programming, which we like to refer to as actually self-talk….what you say when you talk to yourself… is from an Impersonal, Isolated and Impermanent perspective, and what you say to yourself because of your programming would be the opposite of what you think and say in response to a positive event.

When a person is taking a pessimistic approach, however, the programming they employ is completely opposite. When a positive event occurs, they see it as being Impersonal, Isolated and Impermanent ("How did I manage to pull that off? What a fluke! That couldn't happen again in a million years. This is just too good to be true.)

And when a negative event occurs, they see it as being Personal, Pervasive and Permanent ("I'm just the best at screwing things up, aren't I? There I go again! I'll never have any luck.")

So, a "You can do it!-PMA (Positive Mental Attitude) is everything!-Your attitude affects your altitude!" approach to prosperity *is* what we're talking about, but it's not just hype. It's the way the world works…..mind your P's and I's and you'll develop a prosperity consciousness. Note that we're not advocating an unrealistic 'keep smiling even though your house is falling down around you' approach to life, but instead, a realistic assessment of your situation, and doing what you can (and are willing to) do in order to achieve the most positive result you can in any given situation. Does that mean that sometimes you wind up abandoning a plan or an idea because it's clear beyond a shadow of a doubt that it's not going to work? Yes, of course it does.

Part of taking an optimistic approach to events and developing a prosperity consciousness is being aware of what's going on around you and determining where you shouldn't be wasting your efforts as well as where you should be concentrating them. That doesn't mean that you sit idly by and just wait for an obvious and unmistakable 'whack up-side the head' before you take action.

You've likely heard the adage that "when a door closes, a window opens" in regard to life happening to you. In essence, that's true. In practice, it doesn't mean that when a door slams shut, there will be a sudden hurricane-like blast that comes through your window. It's your responsibility to understand that you may have to look closely and notice a slight wisp of a breeze that just makes the window curtain flutter for a brief second.

And taking an optimistic view to events rather than a pessimistic one allows you to learn and develop that responsibility that, once begun, develops exponentially, because being optimistic results in a positive outcome, which makes you more optimistic, which produces a positive outcome, which makes you more optimistic, which…..well you get the idea.

Taking an optimistic approach to what is going on around you is, in fact, a natural state of being. The desire to be a success and enjoy a prosperous life is inherent in the human condition, which means that the 'go with the flow' approach isn't just being passive and letting events and factors determine how you're going to live your life, it's being open to all of the abundance that is all around us.

So, when you meet somebody who is being other than optimistic, consider the idea that they are often working very hard at being a pessimist….expending a lot of effort to ignore the naturally-occurring good stuff. (It's another illustration of the psychological homeostasis idea we discussed previously….that a person needs to 'be right' about what they believe, and will therefore go to great lengths to make their outside environment match their beliefs on the inside.)

To put it simply, making a conscious effort to avoid what is a natural part of being human creates a lot of stress in a person's life, and stress is not part of being prosperous.

Consider the idea of optimist vs. pessimist when understanding concept of hourly vs. commission idea we mentioned. If someone goes into a performance-based work situation with a pessimistic perspective and the kind of negative programming we described, it's pretty much a guarantee that a self-fulfilling prophecy (not making enough money, giving up on one job moving to another, etc…) will present itself. However, approaching your job responsibilities with even the slightest level of optimism, along with an open mind about how the world of business functions, will lead to a different outcome.

When it comes down to it, everybody who works in any situation in which a customer buys a product or service is working for a commission (a percentage of the income the business collects from the customer). Even if a person is paid by the hour, they are, in the final analysis, actually getting paid a commission.

The money that goes into the bank account that makes a paycheck 'good' wasn't just deposited by the business itself. The money was ultimately put there by customers. And the employees of any business who understand that concept, and act accordingly when it comes to customer service and taking a positive, optimistic approach to dealing with customers, will be the most prosperous employees of that business.

"TAKING AN OPTIMISTIC APPROACH TO WHAT IS GOING ON AROUND YOU IS, IN FACT, A NATURAL STATE OF BEING. THE DESIRE TO BE A SUCCESS AND ENJOY A PROSPEROUS LIFE IS INHERENT IN THE HUMAN CONDITION…"

When the natural cycle of volume fluctuation occurs, an astute business owner will take all the steps necessary to keep an employee who is known to be positive and optimistic, and, at the same time, at the first sign of a downturn, will take the necessary step of reducing staff by letting go of those who are not as productive.

Are you thinking that your path to ultimate prosperity will be as the owner of your own business sometime in the future? That's all well and good, providing you understand that it won't come true for you if you spend an inordinate amount of time and effort being an under-performer while you're on somebody else's payroll. Consider yourself as already in business for yourself even if you have made the choice to take a position with a business. Yes, you really are operating a business, it's just that you have elected to have only one customer at the moment…..your employer….and your stated task at this point in your career is to do the best job you can do for that single customer.

If you've never looked at things from the point-of-view mentioned above and you're wondering why you didn't figure it out long ago, don't beat yourself up over it. Often, our programming is due to a lack of exposure to the simplest ideas and not yet developing a global perspective on life and living it prosperously.

Here is a simple idea on global perspective based on statistics and estimates of the world's population as we presently know it to be.

If the entire world were a village consisting of 100 people, and maintaining the proportions of all the people living on earth into that village, you would find:

- 61 Asians
- 11 Europeans
- 14 Americans (North, Central and South)
- 14 Africans

And, in that village there would be:

- 52 Women and 48 Men
- 30 Caucasians and 70 non-Caucasians
- 30 Christians and 70 non-Christians
- 94 Heterosexuals and 6 Homosexuals

And, in your village….6 people would possess 59% of all the wealth in the village, and they would all come from the USA. And:

- 80 would be living in poverty or underemployed
- 70 would be illiterate or semi-illiterate
- 63 would have inadequate sanitation
- 50 would suffer from hunger and malnutrition
- 1 would have a university degree
- 1 would be dying
- 1 would have AIDS
- 2 would be being born (Bringing the population to 101 by year's end)
- 16 would be on line

Yes, having a global perspective on your existence and how you fit in with the rest of the world is an eye-opening experience, isn't it? It makes us mindful of something we like to refer to as the cocoon syndrome. Many of us are, from a practical standpoint, fundamentally exposed only to our own small world early in life…a sort of cocoon…. when it comes to programming and our perspective on things. And, as time goes on, we may or may not discover (or be open to discover) things from a more global perspective, even though it's all there for us to learn about.

Learning to be prosperous is sometimes about coming out of our cocoon and understanding that our programming could be limiting us. Consider this quote from someone you have likely heard of:

"The greatest danger for most of us is not that our aim is too high and we miss it, but that our aim is too low, and we reach it."

Who said that? It was artist, architect and sculptor Michelangelo, who was able to accomplish the things he is best known for…the statue of David, which he worked on from 1501 to 1504, and the art on the ceiling of the Sistine Chapel, which took from 1508 to 1512 to paint… because he understood about the topic of our next segment, which is….

NOTES:

_____

_____

_____

_____

_____

_____

_____

_____

_____

SEGMENT FIVE

PERSISTENCE: IT PAYS OFF IN MORE WAYS THAN ONE

SEGMENT FIVE
PERSISTENCE: IT PAYS OFF IN MORE WAYS THAN ONE

Often, when people consider the idea of persistence, they look at it from the perspective of focusing on one task, and seeing the direct result of being persistent relative to that task only. But, the concept of persistence isn't limited to the perspective of one task only. The effects of someone's persistence, even in what is perceived at the moment as being in a small way, can have a far-reaching effect beyond a person's imagination.

Consider the story of Joshua Chamberlain, a Civil War Union Army officer whose persistence in what seemed at the moment to have only a small effect on an outcome during the battle of Gettysburg, but actually had far-reaching effects that no one, at the moment, or even years after the event, could imagine.

Joshua Chamberlain, like many who served as officers in the Civil War, didn't have a military background before volunteering to serve. He was a school teacher, who, because of his level of education, wound up in a leadership position. And, like many officers in both the Union and Confederate armies, he faced challenge after challenge and loss after loss, while all the time keeping his ever-shrinking company of soldiers together and functioning as a combat unit. At Gettysburg, his orders were to defend only a small segment of the battle line and keep the Confederate troops from overrunning his position.

As the battle wore on, he lost more men and reached a point where his company was desperately low on ammunition. And then things got worse. The Confederate troops, under orders from their commanding officer launched another charge up the hill, determined to break through the small segment of the line that Joshua and his men were assigned to defend. Amid the smoke and noise and rifle mini balls whizzing through the air, the trademark blood-chilling Rebel Yell from the Confederate soldiers charging up the hill pierced the air, and everyone, including Joshua's brother, looked to him for decision on what to do. Their situation was a dire one, and it was clear that they weren't going to be able to hold the line against this last charge.

And, Joshua Chamberlain made a decision. "Form a Great Right Wheel!" he ordered.

Joshua's brother, along with the combat-seasoned sergeant who would be assigned to carry out the order, was aghast, because Joshua's order was for an attack, not a defensive tactic. But, they carried it out, and despite having almost no ammunition, succeeded in capturing the Confederate lieutenant and stopping the advance against their position.

At the time, it looked like it was a very small victory, holding only a small segment of the line of defense, but military strategists, in their study of the battle of Gettysburg, consider it this way: If the Confederate soldiers had broken through Joshua Chamberlain's position, they would have been able to break through in other positions, and breaking through the line of defense would have been the turning point of the battle.

And, winning that battle would have been a turning point in the war for the Confederate Army, allowing them to secure the money they would need for supplies and troops, which would have led them to win the war. With a Confederate rather than a Union army victory, The United States of America would not have come into being as we know it today. The area of North America between Canada and Mexico would have resembled Europe, made up of several different countries.

All of which leads us to World War II. The Axis Powers (Germany, Japan and Italy) were defeated by the countries allied against them, and those allied powers included a "sleeping giant" that was brought into the war on December 7th, 1941 with an attack on Pearl Harbor… the USA, which wouldn't have existed in its current state if Joshua Chamberlain hadn't been persistent in his assignment to maintain a small segment in a line of defense against an army that, had they succeeded in their charge up a hill, would have changed history for an entire world almost eighty years later.

But Joshua Chamberlain's dedication to his assignment, and his persistence in carrying it out, didn't allow that to happen.

No doubt, it's highly unlikely that you'll find yourself in a combat situation, but that doesn't change the point we're making. Persistence is a major component of achieving success in any endeavor, and is a basic tenet of developing and maintaining a prosperity consciousness. And, without a consciousness of prosperity, one can be prosperous, earn the money they want to earn, live in the home they want to own, drive the car they want to drive, and travel to the places they want to see and experience.

Persistence is persistence no matter where it is found. Consider the areas of politics, government, and society:

"NOTHING IN THE WORLD CAN TAKE THE PLACE OF PERSISTENCE. TALENT WILL NOT; NOTHING IS MORE COMMON THAN UNSUCCESSFUL MEN WITH TALENT. EDUCATION WILL NOT; THE WORLD IS FULL OF EDUCATED DERELICTS. PERSISTENCE AND DETERMINATION ALONE ARE OMNIPOTENT. THE SLOGAN 'PRESS ON' HAS SOLVED AND WILL ALWAYS SOLVE THE PROBLEMS OF THE HUMAN RACE."

CALVIN COOLIDGE

Consider sports….

"I'VE FAILED OVER AND OVER AGAIN IN MY LIFE, AND THAT IS WHY I SUCCEED."

MICHAEL JORDAN

Consider business…

"BE LIKE A POSTAGE STAMP. STICK TO IT UNTIL YOU GET THERE."

HARVEY MCKAY

Consider science…

"LET ME TELL YOU THE SECRET THAT HAS LED ME TO MY GOAL. MY STRENGTH LIES SOLELY IN MY TENACITY."

LOUIS PASTEUR

Consider the arts…

"OBSTACLES CANNOT CRUSH ME. EVERY OBSTACLE YIELDS A STERN RESOLVE. HE WHO IS FIXED ON A STAR DOES NOT CHANGE HIS MIND"

LEONARDO DA VINCI

Consider entertainment…

"MOST OF US SERVE OUR IDEALS BY FITS AND STARTS. THE PERSON WHO MAKES A SUCCESS OF LIVING IS THE ONE WHO SEES HIS GOAL STEADILY AND AIMS FOR IT UNSWERVINGLY. THAT IS DEDICATION."

CECIL B. DE MILLE

Consider life and prosperity in general…

"RICHES DO NOT RESPOND TO WISHES. THEY RESPOND ONLY TO DEFINITE PLANS, BACKED BY DEFINITE DESIRES, THROUGH CONSTANT PERSISTENCE."

NAPOLEON HILL

No matter what your profession or field of endeavor, what type of business you are in; no matter what goal you are pursuing, persistence will allow you to achieve the success you desire, and as the title of this segment states, it pays off in more ways than one. Obtaining the material possessions you desire…we'll call them extrinsic benefits… are only one part of success and prosperity. The term extrinsic is often used by educators, who define the grades a student gets on a report as extrinsic, while they also realize that there is an intrinsic benefit from achieving good grades. Intrinsic, simply defined, is the way we feel about something that we have accomplished.

People often volunteer for charity service because of the intrinsic benefits it provides them…it makes them feel good to have done some good for somebody less fortunate than they are. But, understanding intrinsic benefits from a prosperity consciousness perspective goes beyond feeling good about something we have done for others. It's a benefit we experience when we know we have done something good for ourselves. This is not selfishness, it' simply about being human.

As human beings we have an innate desire to enjoy life, and to know that we can continue to enjoy it. When we can afford quality, and we take the time to enjoy it, we are reminded that we will be able to continue to enjoy it. If we decide to invest in comfortable, high-quality, all top-grain leather chairs, and we set aside time to relax in those chairs, we get the intrinsic benefit of the persistence we had in order to achieve the goals we achieved, so we could afford to buy the chairs we wanted.

If we have traveled to foreign countries and brought home souvenirs, we can re-live those trips, and feel good about planning more trips, by taking the time to pause and not just notice, but to also touch or hold, the things we have hanging on our walls or in a display case. Certainly these are material things, but if we understand that the purpose behind buying them and keeping them is the intrinsic benefit we get from having them as possessions, we truly enjoy them.

In a patio area outside our bedroom, we have established a place that has become a sanctuary because of the things we have placed there. There's a hot tub, lawn furniture and a set of wind chimes. These items may not seem to invoke an image of a sanctuary for most people, but they do for us. The wind chimes for example, are manufactured by a company called Gentle Spirits, and although we didn't know it at the time, this company is known for producing not just your average wind chimes, but high quality wind chimes that have a resonance and tone that are a true delight to not just listen to, but experience. Beyond that, though, our wind chimes mean much more than that to us.

We bought them for about $250.00 in a small town in a rural area of Arkansas where we had decided to spend a week in a nearby condo. We were there with another couple, with whom we've been friends for a very long time. Our experiences that week included playing golf at a course, which, believe it or not, only charged $10 a round. If you wanted a cart, it was only an additional $5, and, if you wanted a snack, a hot dog and a beer could be had for a mere $1 each....almost unbelievable when you consider that there are courses near our home where a round of golf is priced near $150.00. There was also a day-long guided fishing trip on the White River, massages at a nearby salon, browsing through antique shops and stores, down-home cooking at a small restaurant nearby, and several nights of live entertainment. All in all, a fun week that afforded an opportunity to create a lot of memories.

Back to the wind chimes…

The small shop in which we purchased them was owned and operated by two young men. And one could think that they would, in rural

Arkansas, be subjected to, less-than-pleasant treatment from their neighbors because they were a couple. If that was happening to them, it wasn't apparent. They were obviously excited and passionate about their small shop that offered quality merchandise to the tourists who visited their small town, and living the life they wanted to live.

The way they approached their life and their business is one of the enjoyable memories (in addition to the time with friends, incredibly inexpensive golf, hot dogs and beer, good food, antique shops, entertainment, and salon visit) that are invoked every time we are in the hot tub near dawn, enjoying a cup of coffee and getting ready to greet the new day, when a slight desert morning breeze comes along and gently persuades those wind chimes to resonate with a medley of tones that seems to go on endlessly.

No matter how many years might go by, those chimes will provide us with an intrinsic benefit; a reminder of our prosperity.

We've all heard about people who are surrounded by their things or their toys, but they are not truly happy. That is because those people have simply not learned to be happy about their things or their toys, and haven't obtained them just because they wanted them for their own well-being. Instead of understanding the process of intrinsic benefits, they may have purchased their things and toys to impress others, or on an impulse to have something just because it is a thing; a philosophy that is diametrically opposed to prosperity. Having prosperity, and living it.

"As human beings we have an innate desire to enjoy life, and to know that we can continue to enjoy it. When we can afford quality, and we take the time to enjoy it, we are reminded that we will be able to continue to enjoy it."

If you have persisted in your efforts to succeed, and decided that you have the necessary resources to purchase an automobile that is beyond the most economical (meaning cheapest) vehicle you can get, and you truly enjoy the Bose audio system, ultra comfortable seats, and smooth ride, you are enjoying the intrinsic benefits of your material possession of a quality automobile. And, when you can purchase a car such as we've described above, there is another intrinsic benefit you gain from it. Peace of mind.

Consider the idea that somebody is limited in their resources and their automobile is many years old with many miles on it. Statistically, a vehicle of this profile will need repairs more frequently than a newer one, which means that chances that it will break down when the driver is on the way to, or home from work one day, or heading to school to pick up the kids, more often than a newer vehicle are beyond just fair.

Getting into a vehicle such as that and wondering every time you turn the ignition whether or not it will start OK, or driving along and seeing another car pulled over to the side of the road due to mechanical trouble, then getting the nagging feeling that you could find yourself in a similar situation quietly erodes a person's peace of mind.

And people often don't realize the stress that is working from within them and robbing them of their true prosperity when these seemingly 'normal' or 'just the way things are' factors are in their subconscious, or barely conscious, thought patterns. Someone who gets the idea that it would be nice to take a thousand-mile vacation tour, but decides not to go because they can't be sure their car will make it, is being robbed of their true prosperity. Somebody who thinks it would be nice to move to a different neighborhood or a larger home, but immediately dismisses the idea as unrealistic because of their belief that they can't afford the higher rent or mortgage payment is being robbed of their true prosperity.

When we are persistent in achieving and accomplishing our objectives, we won't wind up being robbed of our true prosperity because we are missing the intrinsic benefits in life and experiencing a lack of peace of mind.

Persistence was the key in our development of a business several years ago that serves us well today. We decided to establish a niche business to produce, publish and sell video training programs to specific industries, and set about figuring out a way to make it happen. Our first obstacle was that we didn't own, nor did we want to rent, a studio that would be suitable for shooting videos from both a lighting and audio quality perspective. What we did have on our property though, was a 14x20 storage barn that we had built several years before. It was nothing but a concrete slab that we had poured by hand, and the framing, siding and roof that made it a storage building.

You might think that 14x20 is much too small to serve as a viable studio for video production, but we had learned through the experience of seeing a shooting area in another production company that you could actually shoot a video in a space even smaller than that. The first part of our modification plan for our old barn was the required electrical supply for all the lights and other equipment that would be operated during a shoot.

With research done on what would be required to get that accomplished, we were able to run the required electrical service to the building from the power supply that already existed on the property. Next, was finding a way to insulate the building, not only for comfort, but for noise. We dealt with this issue by installing standard Styrofoam insulation, painting it black for lighting purposes, and an indoor/outdoor carpet.

The next step was the designing and building a lighting system that would ensure a top quality visual presentation. Studio lighting systems can be costly, but, through persistence, we found a way to bring the system in at a cost far below normal. Halogen lights purchased at a close-out at a Home Depot for $5 each that were fastened with clamps to an assembly constructed of standard electrical conduit, and wired to standard dimmer switches in order to provide brightness control, still serve as the main studio lighting in our remodeled barn.

The next issue we needed to deal with was finding a way to get the programs shot and edited; something we had no real knowledge about. Nor did we have the equipment necessary to accomplish that task. The solution here was outsourcing. An independent production company (one that we still use today) charges a flat fee for a full day and brings in cameras, additional lighting, and audio equipment necessary to get the shooting accomplished. They also do the final editing, and addition of graphics and titling that is necessary to produce a quality program.

To date, we have produced over 75 video training programs in our studio, some that have been produced under contract with a client, and others that we have produced for our own distribution. The amount of work it took to turn our old barn into a studio and produce the video programs we distribute is a distant memory. But the experience we have today when someone visits our website, clicks to make a purchase, and deposits money into our account, is fresh every time it happens.

Our extrinsic benefit is the revenue we collect, and our intrinsic benefits are the peace of mind we enjoy from a steady income stream, along with knowing that we are enhancing other's lives by providing the information they need to accomplish their life and career goals.

If you're wondering how we managed to finance the barn remodel and other things we needed to get the studio into operation, here's how it happened.

In the contract video production business, once a client has approved a plan for their production in the form of a script outline (which is known as a treatment) the production studio requires a deposit in order to proceed with the project. In our situation, we had secured a production contract and received the deposit, all of which was spent on either the materials we used to accomplish whatever tasks we could do ourselves or paying others to do the things we couldn't do.

Yes, you read it right. We contracted to provide a client with a product before our studio was even complete, and we used their deposit to buy the materials and get the necessary work done on the studio in which the production would take place.

What if things hadn't worked out the way we planned? Then we would have developed an alternate plan to use a different area for shooting the project. The bottom line was that we had made a promise to a client to deliver a product, and we would persist until we were able to fulfill our commitment to that client, doing whatever it took to accomplish that task. And we delivered as we had promised.

Was there some risk involved? Of course there was. There always is. But, while there's nothing that completely eliminates risk, persistence minimizes risk and brings you closer to accomplishing what you have set out to do.

And what you set out to do begins with being open to opportunities that present themselves…remember the door-closing/window-opening approach…in the form of thoughts that lead you to have…..

NOTES:

SEGMENT SIX

IDEAS: EVERYBODY HAS THEM, PROSPEROUS PEOPLE USE THEM

SEGMENT SIX

IDEAS: EVERYBODY HAS THEM, PROSPEROUS PEOPLE USE THEM

People don't often think of a follow-though on the development of ideas as part of prosperity consciousness because often, ideas are dismissed due to a negative rather than positive approach to what is new and different. Consider these two situations:

"The telephone has too many shortcomings to be considered as an effective means of communication."

That quote is from an internal memo of the Western Union Company that was circulated in 1876. It was in response to an idea submitted by Alexander Graham Bell. He presented the idea and details of his invention to Western Union because they were already in the communication business, but they turned it down. Of course, the development of his idea ultimately led to the telephone becoming part of practically every household in America. And today, most of us would be hard-pressed to name ten people we know who don't have a cell phone.

And, as far as the second situation, it was reported around the same time in American history, that the director of the United States Patent Office submitted his resignation and suggested that the office be closed because "there is nothing left to invent." If that report is accurate, we're of the opinion that he should go down in history as one of the most un-prosperous thinkers of all time, considering the fact that since the first patent was issued on July 31, 1790 and signed by President George Washington, the US Patent Office has granted over eight million patents. And patents, of course, come about through ideas…ideas that are born through our thoughts.

Scientific research has shown that the human brain produces approximately 70-thousand thoughts per day. Some of those thoughts, of course, are relative to the day-to-day things that happen to us and the tasks we have to accomplish.

The simple act of driving a car, for example, requires a constant stream of thoughts just to make sure we don't run off the road or crash into another vehicle. The brain is telling our body what to do in anticipation as we look through the windshield, and even telling us what to be aware of when we glance in the rearview mirror to see what is going on behind us. Our thought patterns about the task at hand wind up delivering a veritable bombardment of brain messages to our arm, hand, hip, thigh, leg, and neck muscles, telling us to turn our head, adjust the steering wheel, and step on the gas or the brake, and, if we're driving a standard rather than an automatic, work the clutch and gearshift.

Many of the thoughts that the brain produces, though, are not those kinds of thoughts. They're another kind of thought related to the formulation of a question that begins with the two magic words…"What if…?", which occurs to us when we are being aware of our surroundings, seeing things happening, and being open to not just nearly sleepwalking through life, but always on the lookout for possibilities. Possibility thinking, which is what happens when we are awake/alert/enthusiastic, allows some of those 70-thousand thoughts you have every day turn into ideas.

When you study the biology of the workings of the human brain, the term "synapse" explains things from a strictly technical perspective…

"Chemical synapses are specialized junctions through which neurons signal to each other and to non-neuronal cells such as those in muscles or glands. Chemical synapses allow neurons to form circuits within the central nervous system. They are crucial to the biological computations that underlie perception and thought. They allow the nervous system to connect to and control other systems of the body."

...whew, no wonder biologists and other scientists often look like they're deep in thought when they're trying to figure out if they can make an experiment turn out right.

Kidding aside, though, when people are performing experiments and are, in fact, deep in thought, they are actually helping their brains develop, and help them accomplish more. This process is related to the development of a factor in the human brain known as dendrites. The term dendrite originated in the language of ancient Greek and means "tree" because it describes what a tree looks like with a main trunk with many branches, on which there are developing branches, etc… And like a tree branch, dendrites in the brain grow and become stronger, providing we don't do things that retard their growth.

Alcohol in excess, for example, has been shown to cause the dendrites in the brain to shrink, while on the other hand the process of learning actually causes them to lengthen and grow. And the fact is, for better or worse, the learning you do determines the growth of your dendrites, and in the end, the habitual thought patterns you have. (Refer back to our discussion in Segment 4 on programming and how it determines your outlook on events, and ultimately your attitude toward life.)

The point is, you can allow this learning to happen in a random fashion, or you can decide to allow it to happen the way you want it to. Napoleon Hill, author of the classic <u>Think and Grow Rich</u>, discovered a purposeful approach to what we would refer to as purposeful dendrite development while doing his research for that book. After Andrew Carnegie gave Hill the recommendations he would need to gain access to men that were considered to be successful and literally "captains of their industries", he visited Henry Ford, Thomas Edison, and others.

In one case, when Hill showed up for an appointment, he was told by a secretary that he would have to wait because the man he was scheduled to visit was not available. She said he was "sitting for ideas."

Since purposefully sitting down in an effort to get an idea was something he had never heard of, Hill decided that he would wait as long as he had to in order to get his interview. The man he had the appointment with was Elmer R. Gates, a brilliant scientist far ahead of his time who, in the early 1900s, conducted experiments that clearly proved the concept we readily accept today that is known as the mind/body connection. He also had 43 patents to his name, which proves that his "sitting for ideas" approach was effective.

"POSSIBILITY THINKING, WHICH IS WHAT HAPPENS WHEN WE ARE AWAKE/ALERT/ENTHUSIASTIC, ALLOWS SOME OF THOSE 70-THOUSAND THOUGHTS YOU HAVE EVERY DAY TURN INTO IDEAS."

In an isolated room in which he would carefully regulate the temperature and relative humidity, and even the electrostatic charge of the air, Gates would do not only his purposeful thinking...which he preferred to call a "mentative process" or "psychurgy"...but he also carefully studied how external forces in the environment around a person affects their ability to think and be creative.

To put it simply, Gates believed that people could be creative if they would just put themselves in a comfortable environment, and allowing their pleasant physiology to result in the right frame of mind, they would not only be able to solve challenges they encountered in their personal and professional lives, but also come up with new ideas to benefit themselves, and others as well. It's likely that Gates didn't refer to this simple philosophy as a prosperity consciousness, but that's what it was.

(By the way, on the day that Napoleon Hill visited Gates, he waited for more than two hours, which shows that Hill had also a prosperity consciousness because he understood the concept of persistence…see Segment 5… for his interview with him.)

In Gates' case, he took a deliberate approach to mining his brain for ideas, putting himself in an environment that was free from distractions, allowing his thought patterns to flow, then recording what came to him so he could expand on it later and decide how that idea would help him achieve his goals and accomplish his missions.

Everybody has ideas, but the difference between someone who hasn't yet achieved a prosperity consciousness and someone who has, is that while both experience the foundation of the "what if" occurrence, the prosperity-minded person is the one who finds a way to prevent the loss of a fleeting thought. A fleeting thought, from a biological perspective, can be considered as a synaptic response, which means that something you notice in a seemingly random fashion causes your brain to connect that 'something' to 'something else' you have been doing, thinking about, or working on.

Two things, or events, or factors, or whatever, can, when looked at strictly from a separate point-of-view have nothing to do with each other, but due to the synaptic response in your brain, can be put together to accomplish a task, complete a project, or create something "new".

Inventors are often credited with creating something "new" when in reality, what they have discovered (and followed through on…remember: *Persistence*) is a new combination or order of things that are commonly known and understood from their individual perspective, but haven't been thought of before in the newly presented combination. And people decide not only do they want the invention, they decide they need it.

The late George Carlin, the legendary stand-up comedian who was known for being somewhat cranky in his approach to human behavior and life in general, had his own take on this concept, and once noted "If you nail together two things that have never been nailed together before, some schmuck will buy it from you!"

While Carlin's approach to ideas and inventions at first gives you pause and a chuckle, the reality of his opinion on the subject sets in after you digest his quip, and you realize that he was right. Consider Thomas Edison.

Any student in school beyond the third grade can tell you that Edison is credited with inventing the light bulb. Of course, his invention began with the idea of a filament that would glow and provide light when electricity was applied to it. The challenge he faced through the 10,000 experiments (talk about persistence!) he conducted on this idea was how to keep the filament from burning out too quickly. In attempt after attempt, trying a variety of materials he got closer to his goal of keeping the filament burning, but he was still not achieving the results he needed to make a light bulb a commercially viable thing.

How did he ultimately find the answer to his problem? He took a nap.

It's well-known that Edison didn't clock in at 8AM and clock out at 5PM. His work wasn't done while keeping track of time, and he could be found performing experiments at any time of the day or night, so he would often take a break and nap, then begin again in a short time with a fresh perspective on his project. While working on his light bulb, his napping gave him an image of the process of producing charcoal. How is charcoal related to the invention of a light bulb? Through a synaptic response that allowed Edison to put two seemingly unrelated things together into one entity.

One of the processes related to the production of charcoal is ignition that results in a flame, which is ultimately smothered, minimizing the available oxygen. With the idea of charcoal production in his mind, Edison went back to work and made sure that the area around the wires leading into the glass container was sealed. He then drilled a hole in the glass container and attached a vacuum pump sucking most of the air (and, thereby, the oxygen) out.

When he applied electricity to the filament, it glowed, and it glowed, and it glowed. Edison had found a way to put a carbon material together with a glass container, and apply electricity and a vacuum to it, inventing the light bulb. And while we certainly don't consider the American public and the rest of the world to be schmucks, they did buy it from him.

And, to be sure, the process of ideas coming about via a synaptic response isn't reserved only for captains of industry or those whose work results in changing history and the world with an invention such as the light bulb. A trade school instructor once had an idea to improve the method through which the students in electricity classes performed their lab experiments and accomplished their hands-on projects.

The standard procedure in many schools is to present theory concepts in a classroom setting, then move out to a lab area to work on the hands-on projects on training modules, most of which are quite large. What this instructor wanted was a way to make the hands-on training more compact, allowing it to be accomplished in the classroom along with the theory presentations.

"INVENTORS ARE OFTEN CREDITED WITH CREATING SOMETHING "NEW" WHEN IN REALITY, WHAT THEY HAVE DISCOVERED (AND FOLLOWED THROUGH ON) IS A NEW COMBINATION OR ORDER OF THINGS THAT ARE COMMONLY KNOWN…"

As it happens with ideas that we keep in the back of our minds as we go on with our everyday living, the synaptic response that provided the solution to accomplishing this project came while the instructor happened to be shopping at a Wal-Mart. While wandering through an area that displayed camping equipment and fishing gear, there it was….a large-size tackle box.

The basic characteristic of a tackle box is that it has a main area for storage, and also an upper area that can be opened separately. In the upper area are dividers that make it convenient to store fishing lures, bobbers, or other supplies. With the addition of a hinged Plexiglas cover on top of the main storage area of the box that would serve as a surface to allow the attachment of electrical components with Velcro and the fitting of an electrical power supply connection, along with the divided upper area providing individualized storage compartments, the tackle box wasn't for fishing anymore. It became a lightweight, portable case that students could carry with them and set up in a classroom or lab for practicing wiring and electrical circuit testing and troubleshooting.

People often set limitations on themselves related to thoughts and ideas because they don't believe they have the resources or the education to necessary to make their ideas a reality. That's clearly approaching life from a *lack* consciousness rather than from a *prosperity* consciousness perspective. First, the resources you need to bring a thought along from an idea to a concept, to an actual working thing are all around you. You only need to be open to see those resources. And second, the lack of a formal education accomplished in only what we refer to as academia isn't going to hold anyone back unless they allow it to.

We mentioned Thomas Edison and his inventions earlier. It's common knowledge that he had a limited experience in the form of formal education, yet he achieved tremendous success in his lifetime. At a point in his elementary school education experience, he was sent home with a note from his teacher that said he was "addled" and couldn't learn.

Philo T. Farnsworth is another example. With only a high school education and two years of college, he developed a device known as a dissector tube, which is the basis for all current electronic televisions. He filed for his first television patent in 1927 and is also credited for inventing more than 165 different electrical and electronic devices. What's also true about Farnsworth is that while his parents expected him to be a concert violinist, it became clear early in his life that the thoughts and ideas he had would take him along a different path. At twelve years of age in 1918, he built his first electric motor and subsequently produced an electric washing machine for his family.

What about you? Is there a germ of an idea ruminating in your mind that could make some task you have to perform regularly at work or home be accomplished in less time or in a better way? Or do you have an idea for a business that you could develop into a reality? Maybe you have a hobby that, if you took a purposeful approach to the development of an idea about that hobby, you could turn it into something that you not only enjoy doing, but also earn income from it. When considering the process of ideas, synaptic responses, and the development of dendrite patterns in the brain from a prosperity perspective, there is one fundamental philosophy to remember.

There is veritably an unlimited supply of money all around you, most of it in the possession of others. When you have, and follow through with, an idea that provides value to others, they are willing to give you some of the money they have in exchange for the product or service you provide for them. And the more people you touch and provide value for, the more returns you will receive. Yes, it's just that simple.

But, simple doesn't mean easy. We're not saying that normal happenstance is that you have an idea on Monday, and by Friday millions of people from all over the world are exchanging some of their money with you. What often appears to be an "overnight success" doesn't happen overnight. It takes a willingness to outline a plan for success, and be persistent, optimistic, realistic, and determined in carrying out that plan, sometimes for years before it all comes together and affords a steady income stream.

And, oh, by the way, whenever the subject of an idea tuning into a successful reality is discussed, some people are quick to write off what happened as pure luck, or just being in the right place at the right time. Is it true that luck is sometimes a factor in succeeding in bringing an idea into reality? Yes, it is. And in our experience, the harder we work, the luckier we get.

Often, when people talk about luck, you don't hear what we just stated above, but you do hear people talk about it from many other perspectives, such as something that can be invoked through faith only. In ancient Rome, for example, the pervasive belief was that good luck was a gift from their Goddess Fortuna, and they would receive it providing they went through whatever ritual was necessary in order for her to favor them with good fortune in whatever endeavor they were involved in at the time.

And, throughout time, for other cultures such as the Aztecs, Mayans and the Incas, there were rituals performed that were focused on bringing about good luck. These rituals often included human sacrifice of either volunteers or captured enemies (an example of extremely bad luck for the captured party!), or in some cases, a blood offering in which one would cut themselves and bleed on the god's alter to earn favor.

Today, people may pray for good luck if they look at things from a religious perspective no matter what activity they are engaged in. Take a trip to Las Vegas and spend some time closely observing the way people behave, and you'll likely see someone praying for the wheels of a slot machine to line up just so, or dice to land so that the right numbers come up, or you'll notice them looking up just as they reach for the cards they've been dealt. When it comes to luck in a gambling environment, there are two perspectives of wanting to have good luck. There is the Gambler's Fallacy and the Inverse Gambler's Fallacy.

They both deny the unpredictability of random events. The Gambler's Fallacy is what we've described above. The Inverse Gambler's Fallacy is what somebody is leaning on when they believe that since they haven't had a good hand all night or rolled a seven for several days, they're bound to have some good luck soon because they're "due for a win."

"WHAT OFTEN APPEARS TO BE AN "OVERNIGHT SUCCESS" DOESN'T HAPPEN OVERNIGHT. IT TAKES A WILLINGNESS TO OUTLINE A PLAN FOR SUCCESS, AND BE PERSISTENT, OPTIMISTIC, REALISTIC..."

Or, people, as they have for centuries, may have a keepsake that hope will bring them good luck. Perhaps it's a rabbit's foot (again, something not so lucky for one party in the pursuit of good luck if they happen to be the rabbit) or they may have a lucky shirt they're sure to wear on the day they're hoping for good luck. To be sure, there is a lot of superstitious belief related to people's belief in having good luck, and superstition is not something we endorse. However, we do support the idea that taking a positive approach to life in general can have an effect on a person's "luck."

Luck itself can be a self-fulfilling prophecy even though the blind belief in good luck itself is a false idea. As we mentioned previously in our discussion on both looking at things from a permanent/pervasive/personal or impermanent/isolated/impersonal perspective, and then applying that belief system to all events that occur, being optimistic rather than pessimistic will result in achieving success in any endeavor. Add that to the idea of psychological homeostasis (the driving human need to be 'right' about what we believe to be true, and therefore making things come out the way they do for ourselves, even if it's a negative result), and you can understand and appreciate the idea of making your own luck.

It just makes sense that people who believe in good luck are more satisfied with the way things are going in their lives, and ultimately are just generally in a better mood most of the time. When events, be they good or bad, occur randomly to everyone, a belief in good luck will tip the odds of good things happening in your favor, while a belief in bad luck will have the opposite effect. A term that describes this concept is meme, (pronounced like 'dream') that was coined by author Richard Dawson in his 1976 book The Selfish Gene.

While there is often disagreement as to the specific definition of meme, in general, it is described as an idea that, like a gene, can replicate and evolve, and can be transferred from one person to another, or even from one generation to another. The definition doesn't necessarily dictate that a meme is passed down genetically, though, but more as a means of imitation, becoming a cultural unit that is best described as a value, or pattern of behavior, that is a counterpart of a person's genes, which are passed down physically.

Whatever the proper definition, the concept of the meme of belief in good luck is clearly self-reinforcing. It is all about your thoughts, which lead to your ideas and being open to possibilities about ideas, and we mean ideas that are not just your own, but the ideas and help you get from others in your quest for success in life, which is a concept that prosperous people know and believe to be true because....

NOTES:

_____

_____

_____

_____

_____

SEGMENT SEVEN

BEING AT THE TOP MAY BE LONELY SOMETIMES, BUT GETTING THERE NEVER IS

SEGMENT SEVEN
BEING AT THE TOP MAY BE LONELY SOMETIMES, BUT GETTING THERE NEVER IS

At this moment, we are in a tent in a compound at a private game reserve in South Africa called Entabeni. We are here to photograph and enjoy the lions, hippos, rhinos, and other wild animals that roam freely throughout the entire area, including our camp. The reason we mention where we are and what we are doing is part of the point of this segment.

On this trip, we are part of a group of sixteen people on a guided, four-week tour offered by a company called Grand Circle Tours. It's obviously not a business trip, but instead, is a vacation we want to enjoy. That's our objective. To learn more about the culture of this country and enjoy the learning experience along with the sights, which is just the kind of experience one is supposed to have on a vacation.

But, just because it's a vacation doesn't change the basic principle that is the focus of this segment. One way to explain what we're getting at here is to share with you some information from the welcome letter we received from our tour program director when we arrived in Johannesburg, which is where our trip began.

"You'll be traveling each day with people you don't know. By the end of the trip, you'll know them fairly well. But you probably won't enjoy every person every day. The evergreen qualities of patience, flexibility, humor, and mutual consideration will help everybody have a good time."

To put it simply, the point that Tessa, our guide for the entire time we are here, made in her letter was that the objective, the common goal of every person on the trip is to enjoy their vacation. And the only way that's going to happen for everybody, is if everybody is willing to cooperate with everybody about every detail of the journey. No single person in the group (which will grow to a total of 38 for a two-week period of the tour) will be able to pull it off alone. If one person is difficult, inconsiderate, negative, or angry about last-minute glitches or delays that can happen at any time on a trip that takes the group from camps, to hotels in small towns and larger cities, to airports for regional flights, etc...it will have some effect on the outcome of the trip for everyone else. True, it might only be a small effect in some situations, but it will still get in the way of the common goal of every individual. And this fundamental principle applies to everything in life beyond something as simple as a vacation.

It is by far the most important basic tenet of developing and maintaining a prosperity consciousness, and that's why we've saved it for last. It goes beyond the 'two heads are better than one' approach to solving a particular problem situation, and beyond 'group-think' in developing and bringing a new idea to reality. It can be called an alliance, or it can be thought of as synergy. Or, it can likely be described and explained in more ways than most of us can imagine. And one way it can be labeled is The Mastermind Principle. This isn't a term we coined. It's been used by philosophers and authors for generations.

Author Napoleon Hill is credited with formally introducing this idea relative to achieving success in his 1030's book <u>Think and Grow Rich</u>, in which he described the process as "the coordination of knowledge and effort of two or more people, who work toward a definite purpose, in the spirit of harmony" which can be referred to as a Mastermind Group.

Hill's philosophy has been employed by legions of others who have excelled in their profession, craft, and endeavors in everything from business to politics, to sports. Considering that last category, the name Bruce Jenner comes to mind. Not because he was very different from others who won the Olympic event known as the Decathlon, but because he stated specifically in interviews after he won his gold medal, that he employed a mastermind principle in order to achieve his goal.

It's an interesting way to understand a mastermind approach. Traditionally, the winner of the Decathlon, which is made up of ten track and field contests, is known as the world's greatest athlete, and "athlete" is a singular title of honor that is bestowed on one person and one person alone until another person competes for, and wins the gold medal in the next session of the games. And that's the way most spectators think about it watching the Olympic games view the people who have earned the honor of taking the stage and being awarded a medal; that there is one person alone being identified as a winner in an individual competition.

But, as Jenner pointed out, although only the winning athlete takes the stage to receive a medal, there are other people, and other factors that the athlete understands, that have contributed to the final event of awarding the gold medal.

From our perspective, we consider the principle of mastermind to be available to us in two forms, which we identify as the conscious and subconscious. The conscious element of masterminding is to seek out others who you would like to connect with and meet on a regular basis for the purpose of brainstorming, getting feedback, and helping others in the group achieve their goals. If you are interested in getting involved in a mastermind group with others, there are some simple questions to consider in deciding how and what to do about masterminding.

Are you self-employed? If so, connecting with others who are in the formal approach of regularly scheduled mastermind meetings could be the best fit for you. And you don't need to worry in this day and age if there are enough like individuals in your immediate area that you can connect with to join or form a mastermind group. On-line mastermind alliances can be just as effective as in-person meetings.

Consider Linked In, where professionals from around the world belong to discussion groups that are focused on a variety of industries and businesses. Joining there will give you an opportunity to connect with others. Google Plus is another social networking element that can provide you with an opportunity to expand your network.

Do you work in a specific type of industry? You may benefit from connecting and meeting regularly with others who face exactly the same kinds of issues you deal with in your profession. Of course, you would avoid getting involved with direct competitors in this situation, but that's another benefit of using the Internet to participate in masterminding.

"MASTERMINDING GOES BEYOND THE 'TWO HEADS ARE BETTER THAN ONE' APPROACH TO SOLVING A PARTICULAR PROBLEM SITUATION, AND BEYOND 'GROUP-THINK' IN DEVELOPING AND BRINGING A NEW IDEA TO REALITY."

You could belong to a group of people who are in the same industry as you are, but in different geographic areas, which means you can be more open about presenting issues and problems you want to address.

Do you have limited experience? If that's the case, seek out others who can serve as a mentor. And don't dismiss this idea because you think you might be considered a liability in a group. A fresh approach to an established industry or business can contribute to the growth of others be of as much value as extensive experience can.

Whatever your situation, you can find benefit in, and contribute to the success of others by taking a mastermind approach. And, remember that it works just that way. Joining a mastermind group is a two-way street for everyone. You have to be committed to giving to others as much as you want to benefit from the knowledge, ideas, and encouragement from others.

As with any idea or process, there are many different ways to approach masterminding as a group and running a meeting. Here is one way to consider a meeting can function:

From a true masterminding perspective a mastermind group could have no definitive elected or appointed leader who serves in a regular position of leadership. The position should rotate to each member for one meeting.

The meeting leader reads through the mutually agreed-upon principles of the group. The purpose of this step in each meeting is to reiterate the principles, and to allow an opportunity for members to suggest changes or additions to them. Principles are effectively implemented for each member of the mastermind group when considered in the first person.

Here are some examples of very fundamental principles that could apply to any mastermind group:

I Believe: I believe that the combined intelligence of the mastermind principle creates a source of wisdom far beyond my own.

I Understand: I understand that I can be more successful at creating positive results in my life when I am open to accept ideas from the point-of-view of others.

I Decide: I decide that I trust in the mastermind principle.

I Accept: I believe that the power of the mastermind will respond to my every need, and I am grateful for knowing this truth.

Your group may decide on other guiding principles that are more specific to your profession if the objective is business, or they could address other objectives that your group is formed for, such as a fraternal or service organization.

Once the group principles have been presented, the leader asks for updates from each member on their good news since the last meeting. Sharing your positive experiences and receiving kudos from the other members of the group encourages you and them, and is an important element of mastermind meetings.

The next step in the meeting process is to ask each member what goals they need or want to accomplish in the short term. This allows time for each member to offer advice, information on possible resources, and relay experiences they may have had with similar situations. During this time, members are actually making promises about what they want to accomplish, and will be motivated to persist in their efforts due to sharing the information with others in the group.

Keep in mind that accomplishing any effective meeting means that the intended objectives are accomplished, but it also ends on schedule. It's up to the leader to keep things on track and make sure that the meeting doesn't turn into a waste of time.

Perhaps your approach to masterminding won't be as formal as seeking out a mastermind group that you can join, or forming your own group. If so, consider…..do you have a husband, wife, or life partner that is of like mind with you? How about a brother or sister, or even a good friend or colleague? If so, then you have a mastermind alliance with another person. All it takes from there is to allow it to benefit you (and others) on your path to a prosperous life.

Beyond taking a conscious mastermind approach to life, success, and participating in meetings with others, there is, as we mentioned, the subconscious element of the process. From this perspective, it is best described as going within to connect with a Universal Subconscious that connects us all in order to gain insight, solve problems, and tap into an abundant source of ideas. Depending on your beliefs, this process could be described as a part of the science human development, or being spiritual.

Napoleon Hill commented on a similar approach to this concept by following up on his definition of the Master Mind Principle with the following: "No two minds ever come together without thereby creating a third, invisible, intangible source, which may be likened to a third mind."

By whatever opinion or definition, we can simply say from experience that relaxing and aligning, with what may be described as an invisible source, works.

People often unconsciously tap into what we refer to simply as Source when they find themselves dealing with a difficult decision or situation. There's a reason for feeling that the "I'll sleep on it," approach is effective when trying to decide on the right thing to do. It gives a person an opportunity to relax and let go, and let Source work. And, for some, a more deliberate approach to this idea is meditation, which is really a process of progressive relaxation that allows an individual to tap into Source for insight on what to do about a specific situation, or for assistance in the creative process.

There are, as with anything else in life, a myriad of ways to approach the idea of progressive relaxation and connecting with Source. Here's one approach for you to consider:

Set aside five minutes of uninterruptable time in a quiet environment.

Take a few relaxing breaths, close your eyes and imagine….see yourself standing in front of an elevator. When the doors open silently, you step inside, then turn and face the front.

After the doors close, you look up and note that you are on the tenth floor according to the digital display. The elevator starts moving slowly and purposefully downward and you can observe your descent to the ground floor.

Count to yourself in a consistent rhythm…..9….8…7…6…5…4…3…2…1.

When the doors open silently again, you step out of the elevator and you are in a quiet, dimly-lit room that you realize is a private theater with only one comfortable chair and a flat screen on the wall. The screen is black.

You make yourself comfortable in the chair, and after you take a deep breath and exhale slowly, the screen fades in from black, and what you see is what you need to know and understand. As you observe the images and words that appear, you now know what the right choice is in a decision you need to make….a question that you want answered….a problem that you have been trying to solve….an idea that you need to embark on a new endeavor.

Once you are sure that you have the information you need, the screen fades to black, and you get up from your chair and walk to the elevator. The doors open silently, and you step in and turn to the front. As the doors close, the digital display shows 1, and you follow the purposeful upward progress until the display shows 10, the doors open, and you step out.

And, there you have it. An example of how you can access a wealth of information and advice by masterminding with Source. Combined with masterminding with others you are in harmony with will guide you to embrace a prosperity consciousness.

"Beyond taking a conscious mastermind approach to life, success, and participating in meetings with others, there is, as we mentioned, the subconscious element of the process."

Allowing that consciousness to work for you, all the time understanding the difference between a wish and a serious desire to do, be, and have what you want in life, and committing to investing the time and effort necessary to achieve what you decide to do, along with always keeping in mind that you are willing to give value and opportunity to others will guide you through a prosperous life.

AFTERWORD

ANOTHER NOTE FROM THE AUTHOR

AFTERWORD
ANOTHER NOTE FROM THE AUTHOR

I've been told, sometimes gently, and sometimes not-so-gently, that I have a tendency to be a bit 'windy' sometimes. Peggy often says that if somebody were to ask me what time it was, I would want to tell them how to build a watch before I finally said, "It's eleven-thirty".

Well, while I won't admit completely to 'guilty as charged' I will show some restraint here, saving some of what I wanted to say for my next book. But, as long as we're here, I've got some final thoughts to share….

Not long ago, after checking in one evening into a condo at a resort in Phoenix where we were staying for a week, we decided that dinner would be easy if we just ordered a pizza. When I answered the knock on the door about thirty minutes after calling to place our order, our uniformed, smiling delivery person was there to greet me, introducing himself and letting me know that "dinner's ready"! I judged him to be in his late 50's or early 60's.

And, although I know that many people who do pizza delivery are not comfortable coming inside, I, as I always do, invited him in, figuring it would be easier for him to set his insulated bag down on the kitchen table and slide our pizza out.

After setting the pizza on the table, he showed me and told me about the other things he had brought along…."Here's your paper plates, packets of hot peppers and cheese, and your 2-liter bottle of soda…."in his obviously well-practiced , businesslike tone, and as I handed him the cash to pay the bill along with his 20% tip (yes, I enjoy giving people a 20% tip when we get good service…I believe it's one of the most fundamental prosperity principles), I imagined some things about him.

By the way....Peggy says I "make up stories all the time" because I like to romanticize things. Well, OK. Guilty as charged on that one....

I imagined that he was doing pizza deliveries for more than just the money; that he was retired from whatever his chosen career was and he decided he wanted something to do to stay busy. Do I know if this is all true about him? Well, I didn't interview him for details, but, as he was on his way out the door, he said, "Hey, what more could you ask for? You've got a delicious pizza for dinner, and you're staying at a nice resort," as he looked around and waved his arm about.

And then he paused, looked me square in the eye, and said, "And you deserve it, don't you."

It wasn't a question. And he wasn't surprised when I agreed with him.

I'm sure that he believed he was living a prosperous life. And I'm sure that he understood that he deserved to have, and live prosperity because he followed the necessary fundamental principles that afforded him that opportunity, and I'm sure that you deserve to live a prosperous life too.

Jim Johnson

Prosperity Quotes

"Money is a good servant, but a bad master." Henry George Bohn (1796 – 1884) English Publisher

"The man who damns money has obtained it dishonorably. The man who respects it has earned it." Ayn Rand (1905 -1982) Americal Author

"There are three faithful friends; an old wife, an old dog, and ready money." Benjamin Franklin (1706 – 1790) American Statesman and Publisher

"It is better to have a permanent income than to be fascinating." Oscar Wilde (1854 – 1900) Irish poet, playwright and novelist

"The darkest hour of any man's life is when he sits down to plan how to get money without earning it." Horace Greeley (1811 -1872) American journalist and politician

"I'd like to live like a poor man with lots of money." Pablo Picasso (1881-1973) Spanish painter and sculptor"

"Money, which represents the prose of life, and which is hardly spoken of in parlors without an apology, is, in its effects and laws, as beautiful as roses." Ralph Waldo Emerson (1803-1882) American essayist and poet

"Money is like a sixth sense – and you can't make use of the other five without it." W. Somerset Maugham (1874-1965) English novelist

"The lack of money is the root of all evil." George Bernard Shaw (1856 – 1950) British author and social reformer

"Money bewitches people. They fret for it, and they sweat for it. They devise most ingenious ways to get and most ingenious ways to get rid of it. Money is the only commodity that is good for nothing but to be gotten rid of. It will not feed you, clothe you, shelter you, or amuse you unless you spend it or invest it. People will do almost anything for money, and money will do almost anything for people. Money is a captivating, circulating, masquerading puzzle." Anonymous

"If you don't do it excellently, then don't do it at all. Because if it's not excellent, it won't be profitable or fun, and if you're not in business for fun or profit, what the hell are you doing there? Robert Townsend (1920 – 1998) American business writer and former president, Avis Rent-a-Car, Inc.

"It is a funny thing about life: if you refuse to accept anything but the best, you very often get it." W. Somerset Maugham (1874 -1965) English novelist and dramatist

"We learn wisdom from failure much more than from success; we often discover what we will do by finding out what we will not do; and probably he who never made a mistake never made a discovery." Samuel Smiles (1812 – 1904) Scottish author

"Don't be afraid to take a big step. You can't cross a chasm in two small jumps." David Lloyd George (1863 – 1945) British statesman and Prime Minister

"Being a tightrope is living. Everything else is waiting." Karl Wallenda (1892 -1976) American aerialist and circus performer

"Security is mostly a superstition. It does not exist in nature…..Life is either a daring adventure or nothing." Helen Keller (1880 – 1968) American essayist and lecturer

"Unless you enter the tiger's den, you cannot take the cubs." Japanese proverb

"The greatest mistake you can make in life is to be continually fearing that you will make one." Elbert G. Hubbard (1856 – 1915) American writer

"Behold the turtle. He makes progress only when he sticks his neck out." James Bryant Conant (1893 – 1978) American chemist and educator

"There is only one success –to be able to spend you life in your own way." Christopher Marley (1890 – 1972) American writer

"I am against a homogenized society. I want the cream to rise." Robert Frost (1874 – 1963) American poet

"In the depth of winter, I finally learned that within me there lay an invicible summer." Albert Camus (1930 – 1960) French novelist, essayist, and dramatist

"There is no such thing as accident; it is fate re-named. " Napoleon Boneaparte (1769 – 1821) Emperor of France

"Luck? I don't know anything about luck. I've never banked on it, and I'm afraid of people who do. Luck to me is something else; hard work – and realizing what opportunity is and what isn't." Lucille Ball (1911 – 1989) American actress

"Success is never final." Winston Churchill (1874 – 1965) British statemen and Prime Minister

"No man can claim to be free unless he has a wage that permits him and his family to live in comfort." Sidney Hillman (1887 – 1946) American labor leader

"Whenever I make a bum decision, I just go out and make another." Harry S. Truman (1884 – 1972) 33rd president of the United States

"Be willing to make decisions. That's the most important quality in a good leader. Don't fall victim to what I call the 'ready-aim-aim-aim-aim syndrome' ." T. Boone Pickens (1928 -   ) president, Mesa Petroleum Company

"I've been rich and I've been poor. Rich is better." Sophie Tucker ((1884 – 1966) American actress

"Better to be *nouveau* than never to have been *riche* at all." Anonymous

"I've never been poor, only broke. Being poor is a frame of mind. Being broke is only a temporary situation." Mike Todd (1907 – 1958) American theatrical producer

"Wealth is not without its advantages, and the case to the contrary, although it has often been made, has never proved widely persuasive." John Kenneth Gailbreth (1908 – 2006) American economist

"I have no complex about wealth. I have worked hard for my money, producing things that people need. I believe that the able business leader who creates wealth and employment is more worthy of historical notice than politicians." J.Paul Getty (1892 – 1976) American oil magnate and philanthopist

NOTES:

Prosperity: Having It Living It
How To Be, Do, and Have What You Want In Life

Jim Johnson is prosperous, and he's sure that you deserve to be prosperous too.

Other Books By Jim Johnson

Do Good Do Well: Prospering By Understanding That The Ten Commandments Are Ten Steps To Success In Business

ISBN-13:978-1-937660-04-2

Copyright © 2012 By Jim Johnson
MIE Institute
HC 70 Box 3172
Sahuarita, AZ 85629
www.themieinstitute.com

www.ingramcontent.com/pod-product-compliance
Lightning Source LLC
Chambersburg PA
CBHW070517100426
42743CB00010B/1849